ABOUT THE AUTHOR

A one-man cottage industry, Dr. Bramwell is the creator of the bestselling *Cheeky Guide to Brighton*, host of Brighton's long-running salon, *The Catalyst Club*, and singer-songwriter in the band Oddfellow's Casino. He won a Sony award for his Radio 3 programme *The Haunted Moustache* and Best Comedy and Outstanding Theatre awards for his monologues. *The No.9 Bus to Utopia* started life as a one-man show which has toured the UK and been given as a TEDx talk. Although inordinately proud of being a northerner, David lives in Brighton.

He is a medical man by rumour only.
www.drbramwell.com

THE No.9 BUS
TO UTOPIA

for Dave

We have a shared
dream .... a utopian
future !

DrBrunell

THE No.9 BUS
TO UTOPIA

David Bramwell

unbound

First published in 2014

10 9 8 7 6 5 4 3 2

Unbound

4–7 Manchester Street, Marylebone, London, W1U 2AE

www.unbound.co.uk

Photo credits

p.36 by kind permission of Findhorn Foundation; p.97 by kind permission of
Eamonn McCabe; p.119, 121 photos of Damanhur's Temples of Humankind
by kind permission of the Federation of Damanhur

Typeset by Sam Gray
Art direction by Mecob
Cover design by Matt Chase

A CIP record for this book is available from the British Library

ISBN 978-1-78352-038-1 (*limited edn*)
ISBN 978-1-78352-037-4 (*trade edn*)
ISBN 978-1-78352-036-7 (*ebook*)

Printed and bound in Great Britain by Clays Ltd, St Ives plc

CONTENTS

PROLOGUE – P1

CHAPTER 1 – P3

The Very Important Project

CHAPTER 2 – P9

Losers' Paradise

CHAPTER 3 – P35

The Angel of Findhorn

CHAPTER 4 – P61

A Polyamorous Playground

CHAPTER 5 – P93

In Search of a Man Called
Gorilla Eucalyptus

CHAPTER 6 – P147

The Land of Milk and Honey

CHAPTER 7 – P167

Groundhog Day

CHAPTER 8 – P189

The Golden City

CHAPTER 9 – P203

Castles in the Sand

CHAPTER 10 – P223

Just Your Typical New Age Naked
Small-Town Mountain Community

CHAPTER 11 – P231

The Quiet Revolution

PROLOGUE

Stepping out of my house on a cold, gritty November morning, I bumped into my neighbour Tom – a rare occurrence.

'Morning,' he said, shyly.

'Hi, how are you?' I asked. Tom paused, looking uncomfortable.

'I suppose you've noticed that Julie and the kids haven't been around for a while?' I nodded, not quite telling the truth. I'd noticed it had been quieter next door but that was all.

'She walked out on me six months ago.' He paused again. 'I guess I'm not an easy man to live with.' And with that, he was on his bike and gone. It was our longest conversation in nine years. Only afterwards did it occur to me to say, 'Me too.'

I live in Brighton in a small cul-de-sac, perched on a ver-
tiginous slope in a district known as Hanover. The neighbourhood consists of dozens of streets of multicoloured terraced
houses. It is known affectionately as 'Muesli Mountain' or,
according to one local wit, 'big hair, small houses'. Hanover
has an organic butcher, a pub that sells kangaroo burgers and
a Dr Who obsessive who owns a Tardis and occasionally takes
his K9 for a walk. In 2013 Hanover featured on the satirical
TV show *Have I Got News for You* after a local resident wrote
to the council, claiming that whilst out walking his dog on
Montreal Terrace, he had 'noticed a portal to another dimen-
sion emitting an unsettling yellow light'. He asked the council
if they were going to remove it, complaining that it was
'potentially hazardous'.

While being typically Brighton, Hanover has a reputation
as a friendly neighbourhood. After living there for nearly a
decade however, I still only knew three or four people to nod
hello to in my street. When I first moved in I had thought about
knocking on a few doors and introducing myself, but I didn't.
Instead I kept my head down and went about my business.
After all, it's the city way. We value our privacy, don't we?

CHAPTER I

The Very Important Project

There is a poverty of spirit in modern life.

Carl Gustav Jung

So I decided to take a year off and set myself an important project. It wasn't planned, but when you've been dumped by the love of your life it's either that, sink into depression or enrol for teacher training. Unfortunately I'd already tried the last two after the previous love of my life walked out on me.

Only a fortnight after the bombshell, my ex, with typical expediency, replaced me with someone she described as 'younger but more mature.' He was called Dougal, a name which did, admittedly, help soften the blow. Never again would I warm myself around her naked frame in bed, see her battered old coat hanging by the door, hear the familiar rattle of her hair grips being sucked up by Henry the Hoover or make her

3

giggle by pulling my jogging bottoms up to my nipples and goose-stepping around the bedroom.

She was a kooky Italian who whisked me away on surprise weekends to Europe, bought me clothes, sorted out the bills, cooked Mediterranean dishes every night, picked up treats on the way home from work and dealt with the mortgage. And arranged dinner parties with friends, bought all the food, fed the cat and even wore leather trousers without me ever having to ask.

She was right to leave. I might have been good at making her laugh but it wasn't enough. I spent my time socialising or hidden away in my bedroom studio, making music or writing, occasionally surfacing for food. Family members complained that I never phoned and always seemed to have a good excuse for missing another birthday. If ever I was ill, my ex would stay at home, care for me and shower me with kindness. When she was ill I would grumble until she was better and I could get back to my projects. Looking back, I really could have cleaned out the cat's litter tray more than once. The truth was, I'd been too self-centred, forever wrapped up in myself and my creative projects. I'd lost friendships over this and finally I lost *her*.

For months after the break-up I pottered around at home, keeping myself busy doing DIY botch-jobs and getting emotional whenever any old, cheesy break-up songs came on the radio (once, to my shame, even a song by Phil Collins). Then came a sliver of hope. Out of the blue, my ex called up in tears: she had to see me *that* night. My heart sang. I scrubbed up, shaved, put on my nattiest outfit, changed my mind, donned a different one, then a third. I experimented with hats for a while, for a dash of elegance, but couldn't risk the chance of hat hair. I nervously paced the house, smoking a cigarette and spending the next ten minutes cleaning and re-cleaning my teeth and washing my hands to get rid of its smell – I knew she wouldn't approve. Then the phone rang – it was a friend who I'd been to a gig with the previous night. We chatted for ten minutes, which was followed by more faffing. I finally left the house, spruced up and pungent, and arrived at our rendezvous twenty-five minutes late.

'Typical,' said my ex, cold and teary-eyed, 'I knew you'd never change.' And from that moment whatever chance I'd had was gone.

But the familiar portrayal of a lazy urbanite is only half the story. I *can* knock out a good Sunday roast when push comes to shove. And I'm told I have good legs for a man my age. But wait, there's more. In my twenties, when I should have been researching the decline of steel mining in Pittsburgh for my Geography degree at Coventry Polytechnic, my focus was elsewhere. I pored over Carl Jung, Aleister Crowley and George Gurdjieff, dabbled with psychedelics and, to my mother's dismay, started wearing bangles. I was, as my late friend Ken Campbell put it: 'a seeker'. By my thirties, dissatisfaction with conventional life had led me on some singular journeys of discovery. I had taken part in occult rituals, dabbled with naturism, visited S&M clubs, drunk ayahuasca and endured a ten-day silent meditation retreat in Wales in which I openly wept at the beauty of a banana. In Brighton I spent two years in a cult called the Revolutionary Gnostic Shamans of the Light where each night we'd sit together chanting 'hammmmm saaaaaaaaa', rocking backwards and forwards whilst massaging that mysterious muscle that sits between a gentleman's love eggs and his bum hole, all in some bizarre attempt to wake up our 'real' selves. I gave it up in the end when I began to suspect the Revolutionary Gnostic Shamans of the Light were turning into homophobic conspiracy theorists. But it didn't diminish my role as a seeker.

Dissatisfaction with the norm had even led me to take a holiday from the media. Long ago I turned off the radio in the morning, cancelled the Sunday papers and threw out the telly in an attempt to avoid the toxicity of news. 'Isn't it awful…' was one family member's mantra every time he picked up the paper in the morning, something that must happen in millions of households every day. Without the news I felt liberated from an addiction to a bleak soap opera that recycled the same stories of scandal and brutality, stories designed to fan the flames of our righteous indignation rather than our compassion.

After the break-up with my ex, however, such grand gestures had still not saved me from a classic mid-life crisis. I wallowed in self-pity and talked incessantly to friends about my heartache. I even signed up to Guardian Soulmates, an online dating site that seemed to be occupied exclusively by women who spent their weekends skydiving, snorkelling and standing on top of mountains. To be honest, I'm not really the sporty type. And besides, how can you possibly know if you fancy someone from a picture of them underwater or plummeting through the sky in an inflated boiler suit and goggles? The truth was, I wasn't ready for anyone new. I needed a sea change, an adventure. I needed a project. And as a man needing to escape his suburban existence and painful memories, I chose the ultimate project: to seek out my own Utopia.

As a 'seeker' I'd always been fascinated with 'intentional communities': places outside conventional society that challenged the western lifestyle. Over a number of years I'd unearthed a tantalising list of anarchist communes, sexual utopias and a place in the Alps that sounded like something straight out of a science-fiction film, but I never dreamed I'd ever visit them. Now I had the perfect excuse. Being rather hopeless with foreign languages and traveller's diarrhoea I decided to confine my journey to the West. I would also avoid anywhere that could leave me trapped in a yurt with a bloke called Merlin, shaking a tambourine over my head and humming. I'd experienced enough of that already. And besides, I live in Brighton, a town where it's easier to find someone to clean your chakras than unblock your sink. Instead I would choose the most extraordinary-sounding communities and commit to spending at least a month at each one. And if, at the end of it all, none of them took my fancy, at least I would get *her* out of my system.

There was a more serious side to the project too. I wanted to understand what it was about me that couldn't make a relationship work. I knew I wasn't alone. I'd seen countless friends crash and burn in marriages and long-term relationships in recent years. When the news of my ex and I splitting up reached our friends, one couple we knew were horrified:

'But we put all our hopes in you, you seemed perfect together,' they said, and split up shortly afterwards, as if to make a point.

In America half the population is currently classified as single, with over a quarter living alone. In Europe the numbers are rising dramatically too. Increasingly we seem to be choosing to live on our own. But is it simply a lifestyle choice?

In the West many of us (myself included) have enough money, material comfort and relative freedom, yet few people seem truly happy. I see friends around me popping pills to get them through the day, and these are people with comfortable lives. Anti-depressants are the most prescribed drug in the US and parts of Europe. That in itself is depressing, and yet the media continues to peddle doom and gloom. Is it us, our culture, or our cities that aren't working? Have those living outside society in alternative communities found a better way to live in the twenty-first century? And if so, why do so many of them still insist on wearing tie-dye? I made it my mission to find out. I cashed in my savings, took a year out of my teaching job, cancelled my pilates class and the odyssey began.

CHAPTER 2

Losers' Paradise

Denmark is small country with few interesting places to visit.
As one of the last democratic states smokers are allowed to
pleasure themselves in baby bars. New tourists be warned.
Do not visit Christiania where drug-dealing is good
and lots of crime.

Advert found on Japanese tourist information website

In a 2012 study, the UN's World Happiness Report, Denmark
was declared to be the 'Happiest Country in the World'. The
Swiss, Norwegians and Austrians may have been richer, but
despite the bad weather, long dark winter nights and world's
highest income tax, it was the Danes who were full of the joys
of spring. This was a little surprising. I mean, you'd never
know a Dane was happy. This tall, Nordic race is not renowned
for outward displays of emotion and, thinking about it, their
TV dramas and Lars Von Trier films are hardly a barrel of
laughs either. It was, I could only conclude, an inner sense of
smugness, knowing they're all so tall and damned attractive.
But then measuring happiness is hardly an exact science. Part

of the survey asked how often people saw their family and friends. The Spanish gave this low marks, complaining 'hardly ever, about two or three times a week', while the Danes rated it highly, cheerfully stating 'all the time, about two or three times a week'. And so the Danes were the winners.

There is, however, something unique in the Danish culture relating to happiness. They have a word, *hygge* (pronounced hay-ger), meaning: happy doing nothing, chilling out with friends or alone in a cosy place where the turmoil and troubles of the outside world are forgotten. Or just stoned out of their skulls. The Danes might not be the greatest exporters of art and culture compared to the US or the UK, but perhaps they've been simply too busy enjoying life. As the old French maxim goes: 'happy people don't make history'. Incidentally, in the Happiness Report my nation of grumblers rolled in at 41st, sandwiched between Kazakhstan and Poland. I felt oddly proud, which only goes to show what a self-defeating bunch the English really are.

While the happiest country on earth seemed the perfect starting point for my odyssey, there was something else that drew me to Denmark. Over the last few decades the centre of Copenhagen had been home to an anarchist community: the Freetown of Christiania, a self-styled 'Losers' Paradise'. Like Burgundy in the Ealing comedy *Passport to Pimlico*, it was an independent state in the centre of a European capital city, a hippy version of the Vatican. What's more, it was car-free. I'd never have believed such a place could exist for real. The more I read about Christiania, the more I idealised the place until eventually I was harbouring a fantasy of turning up, fighting for some worthy cause, falling for a tall Danish intellectual and settling down. But then things never do quite work out as you'd planned.

*

The Freetown of Christiania came into existence in the early summer of 1971, when a pioneering squatter discovered eighty-five acres of disused buildings and waterways once occupied by the Danish army north of the river in Copenhagen. The news soon spread with the help of a hippy magazine, bearing the quirky headline *Catch the No.8 Bus to Utopia*. Within a short time a community began to grow, with surprising support from the country's Minister of Defence who called Christiania 'an important social experiment' (thus securing his removal to the backbenches in the next cabinet reshuffle). Christiania was granted a few years' grace, but when the time came to wrap up the party, the residents had other ideas. They barricaded themselves in and pelted the police with stones, bottles and hardback copies of *Jonathan Livingstone Seagull*. For a while, Christiania was left alone and with new-born confidence the residents went into overdrive. Houses were built at an incredible rate along the embankments and in its 'city centre'. A large hangar once used for exercising horses became a live venue and cafés and restaurants were built (vegan, naturally). Christiania even experimented with its own currency, the Fed, the symbol of which was a hash pipe. Back in the Seventies one Fed was worth one medium-sized spliff.

Being an anarchist community, Christiania had just three rules:

1. No hard drugs.
2. No violence.
3. The third is a bit vague but can be summed up as:
   'if you do stuff that really starts to piss everybody
   off, there'll have to be a meeting'.

The Christiania I first encountered was encircled by high stone walls, barracks and waterways. Stepping through the entrance I was confronted with a jumble of huts and wooden shacks. It was hard to believe that a shanty town could exist in such a well-heeled city as Copenhagen. Dirt roads snaked around the buildings, along which the city's trademark tricycles – two front wheels supporting a large box for carrying shopping, bulky goods and small children – would occasionally trundle by, kicking up clouds of dust. There was a town centre of sorts where two of the main tarmac streets formed a crossroads. Here, leather-faced men and women in prehistoric knitwear loitered. A young girl in dungarees was painting a green yin-yang symbol on a boulder. An array of stalls sold the same clichéd ephemera that had been doing the festival circuit for decades: juggling balls, dope-smoking paraphernalia, Native American dreamcatchers and that old postcard favourite, 'I Like the Pope, the Pope Smokes Dope'. Red t-shirts with three yellow circles were ubiquitous, bearing the slogan: 'Bever Christiania' (Free Christiania). At one of the stalls a man with

long grey thinning hair and a stalactite of snot hanging from his nose picked up a guitar and begin to sing. As I listened to him crucify 'Hotel California', a red-faced woman with David Bowie teeth sidled up to me sucking on a joint. I thought she was going to offer it to me, but instead she let rip a terrific fart. A dreadful sinking feeling came over me. I needed a drink.

The Woodstock Bar was like something from the Australian outback. Dogs lazed across benches and floors, pot-bellied men with ponytails, lumberjack shirts and blotchy tattoos stood around guzzling beers and rolling cigarettes. Occasionally a group of them would lurch drunkenly in unison like the crew of the USS *Enterprise* under enemy fire. A peeling poster of the Mona Lisa with a joint dangling from her mouth hung above the bar. 'Hotel California' was playing on the jukebox. The barman, almost toppling over from the weight of his enormous walrus moustache, was handing over my drink when a rumpus kicked off outside. Five policemen were escorting a young kid from the premises only seconds after he'd lit up a joint. A young man with dreadlocks was on his haunches filming it all. The woman with David Bowie teeth appeared next to me and began frothing at the mouth about 'the fucking police'.

'Christiania is the training ground for those new to the police force, which means they're allowed to get shitty with us because they're young and stupid. We film it in case the bastards put the boot in, but recently they've taken to arresting the cameraman too. Cunts.'

Clearly I had made a very big mistake. Christiania was like

Reading High Street on a bad day, populated by Glastonbury casualties. I was ready to call it a day and move on to try my luck in Findhorn, the next community on my list, when another woman spoke to me.

'Hey, David? You are David from Couchsurfing, no?'

Before leaving for Denmark I'd signed up to Couchsurfing.com, a website where people can offer their sofa, floor or spare room for visitors who are new to town and need somewhere to crash for a few days. In return, one can 'couchsurf' anywhere in the world. My couchsurfing experiences back in England, however, hadn't all been plain sailing.

A few weeks before leaving for Christiania, I accommodated a couple of young German girls who were staying in Brighton for the night. I barely saw them as they were in and out the house within minutes, off to explore the city's nightlife. In the morning I found them in my living room flicking through a local guidebook I'd written for Brighton. The short one was reading my 'spoof biography'.

'It says in this book that you have two bum holes. What is *bum hole*?'

'It's your bottom,' I said, pointing at mine.

'And, you have *two*?'

'Yes, eh, well, it's just a joke,' I said. She looked unimpressed. Her companion looked over her shoulder.

'It says here that you also like having sex with animals?'

'I don't. It's just a joke too.'

The tall one looked equally unimpressed.

'Hmm, we go now.'

'Can I give you a lift anywhere?' I said.

'No, we walk,' she said firmly, and the pair picked up their rucksacks and headed straight for the door. In an attempt to cover up the embarrassment I rushed after them – the Beast with Two Bumholes – to wish them *bon voyage* and as I did, I slipped on the rug in my hall. As it slid from under my feet I lost my balance and ended up throwing my arms around the diminutive one and wrestling her to the ground.

'Oh Jesus, I'm sorry,' I stuttered, picking her up. I was relieved to see on the website a few days later that the girls had described me as 'the perfect host, despite having two bottoms'.

While unable to find anyone on Couchsurfing.com to accommodate me in Christiania, I had found someone willing to show me round: Helen, a woman in her early forties who had been a resident there for over twenty years. She was a golden-haired French lady with a long nose, brilliant eyes and an endearing hobble, the result of a recent bicycle accident that had left her with a broken toe. She picked up my disdain for Christiania immediately and whisked me away from the ranting woman at the bar.

'You don't like it here,' Helen stated.

'I have to keep reminding myself I'm not at some terrible New Age festival where someone has spiked my drink with brown acid.'

'You've had the classic tourist experience,' she laughed. 'Now let me show you the other side of Christiania.'

Helen's tour began with her taking me round the old naval

barracks. There were half a dozen or so spread around Christiania, some for accommodation, others housing an assortment
of activities. Kvindesmedien was the workshop for the black-
smiths. Inside, three women in dungarees, cigarettes dangling
from their lips, welded huge strips of iron.

'They started out making stoves from old wheelbarrows
in the Seventies when Christiania had no electricity,' Helen
explained, 'now they make *objets d'art.*'

Another cavernous barrack contained rows of rescued
chairs, doors, windows and electrical goods, precariously
balanced up to the ceiling.

'Every Monday morning a few of our residents scour
Copenhagen's abandoned houses. They strip them and bring
the stuff back to sell. Otherwise it'd all just end up as landfill.
Positive, don't you think?' I had to agree.

We approached a third building, the Grey Hall. An articu-
lated lorry was parked outside. People were lugging PA
equipment into the dark interiors for a warehouse party.

'What kind of music are you playing tonight?' I asked one
of the crew.

'Oh, traditional Greek music, Balkan Folk, you know, that
sort of thing.'

I was surprised.

'I thought it'd be more hardcore dance music?'

'Yes, but the old folk here are not so keen on that so to keep
everyone happy we play this instead.'

I liked the idea that the elderly residents of Christiania
were taken into consideration when it came to throwing a

community party. How different to the club and pub culture of England that increasingly seems to focus on the young. Only a few years previously in Brighton, the local papers had run a story about a man in his forties who had been refused entry to a local trendy pub for being 'too old'.

The community's greener pastures lay a short walk from the centre of Christiania. As Helen and I continued on, dirt roads gave way to tree-lined paths, raised grassy embankments and waterways. We entered the leafy suburbia of Munchkin Tudor, full of hand-built Hobbit homes. Before us stood dozens of curious and sometimes stunning houses, like giant cuckoo clocks, where branches snaked out of window-frames and rooftops curled upwards like Dutch pigtails. Along the embankment were more fairy-tale homes and even a dumpy grey diamond that looked like a crap UFO, abandoned by embarrassed aliens. A large engraved stone lay over a bridge. Helen translated for me: 'In memory of Holger Malmström, 1910–1992, Christiania's best rat-catcher.'

Helen's house was on the very edge of Christiania, on a leafy path adjacent to one of the many waterways that surrounded the community. It was a solid stone and wood two-storey with an open-plan living room and kitchen decorated with artwork. In estate agent language it would have been considered 'a desirable property'.

After a brief tour and a cup of something herbal, Helen proudly showed me her 'bare wall'. It was a nice wall, as walls go, but it wasn't bare. It was painted mustard yellow and decorated with oil paintings. Helen began pointing at several

faint striations under the staircase.

'Look, look, you can still see the scratch marks. It took a long time to get the house cleaned up after the bear moved out. There was so much shit on the floor.'

'Sorry,' I said, confused, 'are you saying that a *bear* once lived here?'

'Of course,' she said, a little hurt that I doubted her. 'We had a lot of animals in Christiania back then. A monkey that danced, lots of parrots, and a snake that' – she looked away as if troubled by a memory – 'that I never cared for. And the bear was called Ricky. You could always recognise her in Christiania, she wore a little tie.'

Helen made it sound as if gangs of bears ambled through Christiania on a daily basis and the only way to recognise Ricky was through her natty attire.

'She was a very sweet bear, but then she began to hang around with musicians. And you know what musicians can be like. Before long Ricky was an alcoholic bear. Aggressive! You know the kind?'

'Er, sort of,' I said.

'She put the man who used to own this house in hospital after a fight over a bottle of wine. I mean, technically, it was not Ricky's bottle to drink but she could get so violent sometimes. After this we knew we had to get rid of her. We tried the zoo but she failed the interview, she was too drunk. Then a neighbour said he had a spare apartment in Verstebro she could go to.'

'Spare apartment?'

'Well she had to live somewhere. But when the taxi came…'

'Taxi?'

'Well, she couldn't walk there, it was miles away. She was so fat by then from all the drink. It took four of us to squeeze her through the door and into the back seat. I never saw her again. That, David, is the story of my bear wall.'

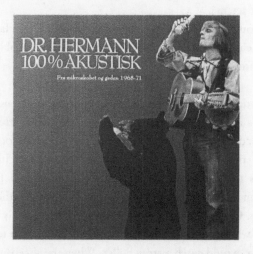

Over the next few days, Helen and I became good friends. She was generous with her time and resources. She treated me to a massage and cooked great vegan curries, which challenged my delicate digestion so that I had to make excuses to 'pop outside to take in a bit of air'. Together we took walks around her quiet neighbourhood and its picturesque houses. We perused an exhibition of 'enema art' in Christiania's Grey Hall (influenced by Jackson Pollock, the artist had squirted paint pellets out of his favourite orifice to make splashes of colour on giant canvases). We watched a fire juggler accidentally set his trousers alight outside a café and witnessed the police make another arrest for possession of cannabis. Against Helen's advice, I walked up to a line of riot police and asked why they were there. They stood unflinching, staring ahead as if they couldn't see me.

'If you'd stayed a minute longer they would have laid into you,' Helen said. 'Drugs have caused so many problems in our community.'

In Christiania there are no landlords, no rents to pay, no house numbers and no street names except one: Pusher Street. For decades, drugs were openly sold from stalls by the Woodstock Bar. By the Eighties, dealing had become such a lucrative business that two rival drug gangs – Bandits and Bullshit (pronounced *bull-sheeet*) – began to fight each other over territory. Christiania became a warzone. Occasionally a poor tourist, whose only mistake was to have wandered in to buy a bandana, would catch a stray bullet. When the sliced-up body of a member of Bullshit was found under one of the houses, the community knew they had to act. They sealed their entrances and set up a 'Junk Blockade' to keep the junkies and dealers out. It was too late – the authorities came down hard. Police set up patrols around Christiania every few hours. Anyone caught with so much as a joint was liable to get rough treatment. Some still managed to find humour in this. One of the community's cafés still carries the sign:

'Welcome to the Moonfisher. More than six thousand police inspections since March 2004. The World's Safest Café!'

As well as the issues with recreational drugs, I couldn't help but notice what an enormous problem alcohol was in the community too. Christiania was a sanctuary of sorts for many of Copenhagen's troubled souls and addicts who drifted around its streets, making the centre feel edgy and, at times, unsafe. In fact this, combined with the heavy influx of tourists, made it difficult to get a sense of who the real residents were. Helen recognised that Christiania was not the Utopia she had once dreamed of, but remained convinced that life in the Freetown was more liberating and communal than anything Copenhagen could offer. With all the aggro, drug problems and tourists I wasn't sure I could concur.

One of the people Helen wanted me to meet was Britta, the 'great-grandmother of Christiania', who lived in a large green wooden-slatted house in the heart of the community.

'Check for dogs,' Helen warned as I opened the gate. 'You will fight them off with a stick if they come, yes?'

'Er, yes,' I said, quietly hoping it'd never come to that. Instead, we were greeted by 'Hoppalong', a loping Danish man with distillery breath and a dead cigarette that dangled from his lips. He danced around the garden, his floppy hair swinging around like a shampoo advert for the elderly.

'Britta? Yaaa. She asleep. Come back later.' But as he spoke an upstairs window in the house opened and a bleary-eyed woman, tangled up in Wurzel Gummidge hair and a linen nightdress, shouted down:

'If it's your Englishman friend tell him I'm too tired to see him but to watch this.' She threw down a DVD to me and closed the window.

The film was called *Christiania, You Have My Heart* and had been made by Britta's partner Nils. It was an earnest, if overly sentimental, history of the community, which began with clips of happy schoolchildren in a classroom singing the Christiania anthem. Its lyrics included the line: 'People are filled with shit about us, thousands are taught to hate our guts without knowing who we are'. Later on, a young girl painting a mandala turned to the camera and said: 'I, Badger, have found one end of the rainbow at Christiania.' The film concluded with footage of riot police storming a house and then running for cover under a shower of stones and a tirade of abuse. One joker, following the police out of Christiania with a broom, swept up after them. While a little hackneyed, the film demonstrated the tenacity and humour of the residents, who had built their community from nothing despite the ever-looming threat of dissolution. After watching this together with Helen, I began to realise that she had devoted her last few days to me. Helen probably had her own life to get on with after all. I asked if there was anything I could give her in return.

'I'm fine, but a friend of mine needs help. I shall introduce you to Henrik.'

Henrik was a musician in his late forties with a cheerful face and mop of unruly hair. He had lived in Christiania for more than thirty years and was in the process of digging up his living room, laying a new floor and building a new kitchen.

But Henrik had no need to call in the professionals: living in Christiania he had friends and neighbours who were willing to help for free. With a big smile he handed me a box of plumbing tools. I looked blankly at it. I knew as much about plumbing as the average nine year old. Smiling, Henrik shook his head and gave me a box of carpentry tools instead.

'What did they teach you, Restless Englishman? You'll be telling me next you don't know how to lay a floor?'

'Erm...'

He finally found a job I *could* do: ride his Christiania bicycle back and forth to the dump as we removed piles of bricks and dirt from his house. In a place where cars were forbidden, the bicycle was Christiania's equivalent to the Dodge. To manoeuvre round a sharp corner with a heavy load I had to pedal like buggery and twist the handlebars a sharp ninety degrees. Just as one of the front wheels left the ground and I felt certain the bike was going to topple over and eject me, and half a ton of bricks, into a pile of nettles, it would always collapse back onto all three wheels. Well, nearly always.

Henrik's house was part of an untidy horseshoe of twelve rural residences, in and out of which continually wandered friends, children, cats, dogs and the occasional chicken. Working as a composer of music for adverts, Henrik seemed an unlikely soul to inhabit Christiania, but when I mentioned this to him he just shrugged.

'Look around David, it's more free here than in the damned city. Decisions are not made on money and backhanders like the outside world. Of course an anarchist community has its downside, getting a few hundred people to agree on anything is never going to happen quickly. Change is slow but that's how we like it.'

'So how do you deal with problems? What if someone really does start to piss everyone off?' I asked.

Henrik lowered his voice. 'We do what the Romans used to do, banish them. But to be honest the most common problem here now is alcoholism. It's not so much someone irritating us as neighbours getting concerned because their friends are drinking too much or showing signs of depression. Then we work together on how to support these individuals. We make sure they're not alone in their suffering.' It seemed that the community's self-deprecating moniker, 'Loser's Paradise', was not without reason.

One morning, as Henrik and I were standing around in his half-built kitchen covered in dust, a man dressed in tie-dye came bounding down the path to the house, clutching three large canvasses.

'Oh fuck, Herman the German,' Henrik muttered. Herman ducked through the archway that led into the new kitchen.

'You will welcome me in for beer my friend when you hear my news!' bellowed Herman. Henrik raised an eyebrow at me. 'Henrik, I was in my loft yesterday and I found these! Do you remember painting them?' As he turned the paintings around – a trio of action paintings – a flash of recognition passed over Henrik's face.

'I bet you had forgotten all about them,' said Herman excitedly, 'they have been in my loft for years, man! And now I have returned them to you, you will welcome me in for a beer, no?'

Henrik remained expressionless.

'Actually Herman, I hadn't forgotten. I was thinking about them only today. But where are the other two? I left five at your house for you to look after.'

'Oh,' said Herman, crushed.

'You will go back and look please, won't you?' said Henrik. 'I'd hate to think you'd lost them. Then we can drink beer and catch up!' As Herman scuttled off into the distance, Henrik roared with laughter.

'It's nice to see these pictures again after all these years,' he said, 'but I could not face an afternoon with that boring man. He will not dare return until he's found the others. And that might take a long time.'

'Because?'

'Because, David, I only painted three.'

In the early evenings after a hard day's graft Henrik and I, together with his dusty group of helpers, would head across to Christiania's bath house, hot tubs and steam room to get clean and relax. Classical music was piped in throughout, mainly Wagner, a favourite of the attendant who worked there. Naked, we would take to the waters. My happiest times in Christiania were spent in these warm waters, just hanging out and eavesdropping on conversations. It soon became clear that the hot tubs were where the real decisions about Christiania were made, not at the weekly Friday night meetings when four hundred anarchists would sit in a circle in a vain attempt to come to mutual agreement about *anything*. Conversations were animated and open. It was here that a pair of wise old birds with skin like sundried tomatoes patiently explained Christiania's long and troubled history to me, while a fat Swedish woman put her hand on my thigh and whispered into my ear that she'd found a scorpion under her bed.

The hot tubs were also a popular haunt for the old-timers, who spent the evenings reminiscing about the 'glory days'. Back in the Seventies, many of them had been involved with Solväggen ('sun wagon'), Christiania's theatre group, renowned for its political pranks. Their most celebrated stunt took place in the winter of 1974, when Solväggen mobilised an army of two hundred Santas, marched into the centre of Copenhagen with a giant papier mâché goose and began liberating goods from the city's two largest department stores. TVs, food hampers, bicycles, cameras and toys were stuffed in sacks, taken into the streets and handed out to the poor and needy. The shop staff could not overpower them; there were just too many Santas. By the time the police were called, they'd half-emptied the stores. Christiania was heavily fined for the prank but it had the last laugh: in 2004, a film of the Father Christmas Army was voted as one of Denmark's ten most important works of art of the twentieth century. I don't know if this says more about the originality of Christiania or that the Danes have spent way too much time perfecting pastries.

Each night after our trip to the bath house, Henrik would make a fire by the water near his home. Here we'd sit, beers in hands, staring into the flames. I enjoyed these peaceful

moments of reflection, something that had been lacking in my previous life. Sometimes however, there was precious little silence, owing to my need to offload on Henrik my relationship break-up, heartache and the journey I'd sent myself on. He never offered his advice or judgement, just listened with a gentle smile on his face. I probably bored him senseless with it all. One night, after we'd been sitting in silence, looking up at the stars and feeling the warmth of the fire in our bones, Henrik put his arm around my shoulder.

'Tonight, my friend, you seem to have lost some of that restlessness. You seem happy just sitting there, yes?' I nodded in agreement. 'You know what that is, my friend. That is hygge.'

After a week my job had come to an end. The kitchen and floor were complete and Henrik, while demonstrative with his gratitude, was now immersed in a new job, creating music for a shampoo commercial. Like Helen, he had his life to get on with.

Over the next couple of days, at a loose end, I began sliding into bad habits. I shared a joint with a Moroccan tourist one afternoon in the small park by the Moonfisher Café, each of us keeping alert for the cops (a task that gets harder the more stoned you become). The drug put me in a maudlin mood. Without a job, I'd lost my sense of purpose. I felt like I was turning into one of the lost souls who drifted around Christiania's fringes with no place to go. And then I realised: I was. It was time to move on.

*

On the evening before my departure, Helen took me out to show me 'the best bird's-eye view of the city'. Together we climbed to the summit of the Church of Our Saviour – a chocolate and gold-twisted spire with an external staircase – to watch the sunset. Ascending the *outside* of a church spire was an altogether new and terrifying experience, particularly as the handrail appeared to get lower the closer we got to the top. Helen left me there to savour the panoramic view. We hugged goodbye and as she descended the metal stairs I fleetingly caught her scent: joss-sticks, sandalwood, campfires and marijuana. It was the smell of Christiania. I leaned over the tiny balcony, knees shaking, for a final look at the Freetown.

Many of Copenhagen's residents seemed to regard Christiania with disdain; others accused the community of abandoning its principles. One satirical TV show sent a journalist into the suburbs to build a small wooden hut, following Christiania's tenet that anyone could join. Within minutes the journalist was told that if he wanted to live in the community it would have to be agreed by a committee, which could take up to two years. The show levelled charges of hypocrisy. Christiania, it concluded, had become a community of inverted snobs.

Perhaps Christiania was like Gloria Swanson in *Sunset Boulevard*: a sozzled old actress living off the former glories of her youth. After years of legal battles over ownership of the land, Christiania had been forced to pay rent to the government since 2011. It was another point gained by the authorities in a long battle for the normalisation of Christiania. And yet against all odds she remained. Her citizens were an embattled species in need of a little tenderness, someone to embrace them and say, 'You did it. You're still here. Well done, you old buggers.' And while attracting such undesirables as drug dealers, criminals, and amateur folk musicians, Christiania had once been a place where anyone could build what they liked and live how they pleased. But there was something else I learned from Christiania. Unable to find any long-term accommodation in Christiania, these past few weeks I had been living in Copenhagen and cycled back there every night. In those dark hours when my insomnia would flare up, I'd stare out across the street into the lives of the other night owls, alone in their solitary apartments. I gave them all names. There was Travis Bickle, The Pacing Girl, Text Addict and For-goodness-sake-put-some-trousers-on. Not once did I see them leave their cells, knock on a neighbour's door and pop in for a coffee. How different from Christiania, where residents wandered in and out of each other's houses day and night, leaving their doors unlocked and helping their neighbours. The people I had met had heated debates about their community, staged outdoor events and took to the streets to protest against the injustices of the world. They wandered around in open-toed sandals and didn't give a monkey's about celebrity culture.

Since meeting Helen on my first day, there had been a slow but growing realisation that Christiania had been born out of Copenhagen's reserve. Helen had shown me the real Christiania, the side of the community that tourists probably never see. Christiania personified the festival spirit. She was the joker in the pack, the fool to Copenhagen's king. But she could never be my Utopia. This wasn't my world and these weren't my people. There is only so much rainbow knitwear, batik

artwork and yin-yang t-shirts a man like me can endure. Standing at the top of the church that evening, any lingering doubts I may have had were dispelled by a distant melody from the Freetown far below me. Drifting up from the hippy metropolis like smoke curling from a fire was the sound of 'Hotel California'.

CHAPTER 3

The Angel of Findhorn

An hour's drive east of Inverness lays the windy bay of Findhorn, a sleepy fishing village whose peace is shattered every
twenty minutes or so by the screams of jets from the local RAF
base. A few miles south from here is the town of Forres, home
to the faded glory of a Victorian hotel, Cluny Hill. It was here
in 1958 that a trio of middle-aged spiritualists, ex-RAF man
Peter Caddy, his wife Eileen and friend Dorothy McClean,
were employed to reverse the ailing fortunes of the old hotel.
While knowledgeable in all things supernatural, the trio had
little experience in running a hotel, leading Peter to encourage
his wife to seek guidance from God. It seemed to work. Pretty
soon every problem the trio encountered – from how much to

Dorothy, Peter and Eileen

pay the staff to dealing with a *Fawlty Towers*-style alcoholic chef – was solved with God's help.

Through their endeavours Peter, Eileen and Dorothy began to rebuild the popularity of Cluny Hill, with the local press dubbing it the Heavenly Hotel. Its owners, however, were less impressed with the trio's unconventional methods and behaviour. Things came to a head one night when, allegedly, they were outside 'waiting for aliens to arrive' instead of serving drinks to guests and were subsequently dismissed for being 'just *too* weird'.

In the early winter of 1962, the trio (plus Peter and Eileen's three children) moved into a small caravan in Findhorn's caravan park with plans to move on as soon as they could afford it. Eileen, however, was receiving new instructions from God but was unable to decipher His word because of the noise in the caravan and the jets screaming overhead. She asked if He had any ideas for somewhere quieter for her to 'tune in'. Being God, He did, and suggested the caravan site's municipal toilets between the hours of four and six in the morning. Dutifully Eileen went and sat on the cold loo each day awaiting instructions. God's will was thus:

'Build a magic garden,' He said, 'and they will come. One day this will become a great community: a city of light.'

All plans for escaping the caravan site were abandoned and the trio set to work, with Peter toiling in the caravan park's garden and Eileen sitting on the loo awaiting the latest instalment from God. Dorothy, not wanting to be left out of all the excitement, made contact with the spirit of a pea.

'I can speak to you human,' it said. 'You have come
to my awareness. Our life is for the good; but man is
making mincemeat of all life forces. If they were on
the straight course of what is to be done, we could
co-operate with them.'

From *The Magic of Findhorn*, Paul Hawken

Despite the pea's cynical view of humanity, with patience
Dorothy gained the trust of these plant spirits and found that
she could ask them directly for advice. She referred to them
as *devas* (a Hindu word meaning 'beings of light') and was
soon having conversations with dwarf bean devas, rose devas,
spinach devas and tomato devas in the garden, which went
something like this:

Dorothy: How are the tomatoes?
Tomato Deva: It is too cold for them today, but we shall try
to protect. You can give them liquid manure in a few hours.
Spinach Deva: If you want strong natural growth of the
leaf, the plants will have to be wider apart. By leaving them
as they are, you will get overall as much bulk in the leaf
but with not as strong a life force.

From *The Magic of Findhorn*, Paul Hawken

The devas were offering practical but essential gardening tips.
By late spring the gang had over a hundred vegetables, herbs
and fruit growing in abundance. Amazed visitors started
to drop by as stories circulated the village of carrots the size of

a Labrador's leg and tomatoes as big as a schoolboy's head. The group had synthesised the energies of God, devas and mankind in the caravan park. The Magic Garden was in full bloom.

A further addition to the group came in 1965 with the arrival of an elderly gentleman called Roc (Robert Ogilvie Crombie). A retired scientist living in Edinburgh, Roc had encountered the god Pan one afternoon on a visit to the city's Botanical Gardens. Apparently the God of the Wild was suspicious of humankind and full of questions.

> 'Why are human beings so stupid? What are the strange coverings you have? Why do you not go about in your natural state as I do? Why do you go dashing about in boxes on wheels sometimes bumping into each other? Is it a game?'
>
> From *The Magic of Findhorn,* Paul Hawken

While understanding the concept of wheels and boxes, the God of the Wild was clearly flummoxed by motorised transport and clothes. Roc found the trio to be kindred spirits, sympathetic with his visions, and encounters with grumpy woodland folk soon became a popular topic of conversation at Findhorn. Later, when visitors were taken to a local beauty spot, Randolph's Leap, many claimed to have seen visions of fairies there.

By the late sixties, Findhorn's Magic Garden was attracting volunteers and a growing number of people who wanted to live there. The fledgling community soon became part of the hippy trail, though Peter Caddy was less than sympathetic to the frivolities, marijuana and free love that the hippies brought to Findhorn. Clashes between these two worlds meant that young visitors rarely stuck around for long, until the arrival of an American, David Spangler. Spangler's zeal and openness bridged the gap between Findhorn's founders and the hippies. He breathed new life into the place, lecturing in the park and devising courses such as Experience Week, offering newcomers the chance to get a feel for community life there. Through these courses, money started to pour into Findhorn and the community continued to grow. By the mid-seventies the caravan site, acres of nearby land and the Cluny Hill Hotel from which the trio had been sacked became their property.

The eighties and nineties were a time of transition. Either Findhorn had outgrown most of its creators or they'd outgrown it: Spangler moved back to the US and took Dorothy with him. Peter Caddy left his wife for a young German girlfriend and moved to Hawaii. Of the original founders, only Eileen remained, squirrelled away in the depths of the park, a frail old woman, now curiously at odds with the place she had helped build.

Talk of direct communion with devas, angels and God may have diminished over the years, but Findhorn claims to have never lost its sense of purpose: to celebrate and respect the idea that God is within all of us and nature is to be honoured and worked with, not against. Nowadays the majority of Findhorn's residents live in the Foundation: the site of the old caravan park, enclosed on two sides by the bay and a coastline of sand dunes. Most of the caravans have been replaced by beautiful eco-houses, courses run all year round, and over six hundred full-time residents live in the community. Findhorn's focus is now on environmental issues, sustainability, recycling and sharing.

Since Eileen's death in 2006, her toilet in the caravan park has been kept for posterity and is known as 'Eileen's Throne'. Zealous visitors still make pilgrimages to Findhorn to see it, along with the original caravan the trio once lived in, which has been lovingly preserved and given a plaque: 'Original Caravan'. If the *Carry On* team had done *Carry On up the Commune*, they couldn't have done it better than the real thing: the unlikely story of how a windswept caravan site became a flourishing New Age commune thanks to an ex-RAF pilot and his wife, who received messages from God in the site's municipal toilets. As a seeker, how could I resist such a place?

As my taxi turned into the long, tree-swept drive and I saw Cluny Hill Hotel, it was love at first sight. Surrounded by woodlands and a golf course, Cluny was the perfect setting for an Agatha Christie-style 'murder most horrid'. At considerable expense, I had signed up for the long-running Experience Week course in the hope of getting a taste of community life. On a table in one corner of the hotel's hallway was an array of Eileen's books: *The Dawn of Change*, *Flight to Freedom* and *Beyond*. I thumbed through a few. The prose had a biblical flavour to it, mixed with New Age sentiments.

The hotel décor was 'Cluny through the ages': original Victorian wood panelling, Art Deco mirrors, psychedelic carpets and chintzy avocado bathroom suites. Juxtaposed with these were the 'Findhorn' touches – the unicorn tapestry in the ballroom and paintings of ethereal bodies on the walls. Glass cabinets in the hallway showcased books on astroshamanism, alongside bizarre tableaux of toy bunnies sitting on coloured eggs and squirrels clutching pine cones. There were three floors to the building, over a hundred rooms, a sauna, meditation hall, ballroom and a dining room with towering windows that overlooked the forest. Noticeboards bore advertisements for holistic massages and healing yoga. One poster bore a picture of some picnic tables with the message: 'Hurrah, we have manifested three picnic benches!' In the dining room a plaque read: 'We intend to create a welcoming, healing, uplifting energy here with the Angel of Delight'. In the lounge hung pictures of Findhorn's founding members. Eileen and Dorothy looked like sweet middle-aged ladies with owl glasses and permed hair. Peter, a rugged, handsome man, stood atop a mountain with a faraway look in his eyes.

*

I have to be honest, I was half expecting my roommate at Cluny Hill to be a gentle vegetarian called Cosmo, sporting a ponytail and linen trousers. I was so wrong. Carel was the bassist for a Belgian metal band and had short, cropped hair and a wild Jack Nicholson look in his eye. He was, in his own words, 'having a mid-life crisis' until one weekend on a bender of dope and speed a dolphin had told him to come to Find-horn. He was lying on his bed in just a pair of pants and a vest and fondling a Zippo lighter as I entered the room. An old wooden walking stick was resting against the wall. Carel's opening gambit: 'Hey, roommate, do you mind if I smoke in bed?' seemed to be a rhetorical question as he lit up seconds later and threw me a cheeky grin.

My fellow 'Experience Weekers' were brought together later that morning in Cluny's Beech Room by our focaliser Georgette, a short, attractive Brazilian. Among the group was Shirley from Australia, a retired yoga teacher who dozed off after ten minutes; Ann, a sad-looking Danish woman who gently nodded as she spoke and Wim, a spirited Dutchman who, judging from his zeal, was the boy at school who always had his hand up first. Next to Wim sat a white Zimbabwean. His smooth bald head and pointed nose gave him the appearance of a Bond villain, but he had the silky voice of a Mills and Boon hero. We each took it in turns to take part in that time-honoured ritual: 'say-something-about-your-self-and-why-you're-here'. Carel revealed his open-hearted honesty by sharing with the group a few home truths about his relationship break-up and consequent breakdown, which put my rehearsed two-minute monologue to shame. As a group everyone looked rather conservative. I wondered if I'd have *anything* in common with these people. Apart from Carel, I doubted any of them would have a good record collection for starters.

Experience Week was divided up into activities, games, out-ings and daily work duties. I opted for gardening, keen to see the Magic Garden and spend time in the park, the main site of Findhorn, which stretched over thirty acres.

As our bus dropped us off the next morning at the park entrance, I took a walk around the area. A single street led through the site from the main road to sand dunes and the sea beyond. Dotted along it were old caravans, chalets, shops and the dining hall. Near the end of the road lay the Universal Hall, an impressive pentagonal structure full of colour and light, which served as the Arts Centre.

Our gardening focaliser was a seven-foot giant called Liam. He had downy fluff on his chin, rosy cherubic cheeks and soft baby curls on his head. I was astonished when he told me he was twenty-seven. If I'd been a pub landlord I'd have made him sit outside with a glass of Tizer. Before beginning our first gardening activity, Liam brought us together to attune.

Attunement was unique to Findhorn. At the beginning of all group activities we were required to hold hands (right hand up, left hand down: 'the Findhorn Way'), close our eyes and 'tune in' to the task at hand. After a minute of silence Liam said:

'And how do we all feel today? Let's use a weather metaphor. David?'

'Er, cloudy with outbreaks of sunshine?' I suggested.

'Good. Wim?'

'Blue sky man.'

'Good. Carel?' Carel shook his head.

'No, I don't like this cheesy metaphor,' he said cheekily, waving his stick in the air, 'let us do rock songs. I am Iron Maiden, Number of Beast.' The cherubic giant nodded sagely.

Work at Findhorn was partly an exercise in anthropomorphism. The previous day, on the tour of the kitchens at Cluny, we had been introduced to the cooker, Mount Vesuvius, Leonardo the dishwasher and the wall heater, Sam. In the Magic Garden the smiley-faced wheelbarrows, Mr Magic and Willy, were our companions as Carel and I trundled back and forth weeding, cleaning and planting. Giving each tool a personality and name, we were told, offered a greater inclination to treat them with kindness. I thought of my red Henry Hoover back home, who I'd occasionally pat on the head after a particularly satisfying spot of cleaning and whisper 'good old Henry' if no one was watching. And then there was my knackered old printer who'd get the finger every time there was a paper jam. I made a mental note to be less aggressive towards it.

The gardening was satisfying but I was disappointed to discover the plants were of sobering proportions. Where were the giant kidney beans and enormous parsnips I'd heard so much about? When I mentioned this to Liam he said:

'We concentrate our energies elsewhere in Findhorn these days', to which Carel chipped in:

'So you all have enormous cocks?'

*

By the third day I began to loosen up and enjoy the company of the group. A morning of dancing turned out to be enormous fun, as we whirled around performing complex Scottish wedding reels and jigs, swapping partners and snaking in and around each other until our focaliser brought it to a close. We squeezed hands, 'tuned out' and I had that rare delight of feeling genuinely ravenous just before mealtime.

An afternoon of games turned out to be one of the highlights of the week for many of us. In Cluny's ballroom, barefooted, we played blindfolded games of trust as different partners guided us around the room at varying speeds. Holding hands so we were linked in a spiral, we coiled together into one great breathing entity. Later we were planets reaching out to form clusters and galaxies. For one activity, eyes closed, we explored a stranger's hands. My partner's were sensual and searching. They belonged to Masako; so different from the shy Japanese girl who had barely spoken since she arrived.

One morning, a trip was organised to visit Randolph's

Leap, a nearby geological wonder. In a sun-drenched opening in the woodland by the river our focaliser gathered the seventeen of us together to hold hands in a circle.

'Be attuned with nature here. Some say the veil between this world and the next is thin. There may be some amongst you who are susceptible to experiencing nature spirits.'

This was a far cry from the Findhorn of old that I had read about. No more were Experience Weekers being asked to keep a watchful eye for fairies and angels that frolicked and pranced in the woods. Nowadays it seemed to be the overactive imaginations of visitors that kept this concept of Findhorn alive, rather than the residents themselves.

I walked the paths that ran along the black swirling river with Rina, a sweet-natured Australian in her mid-fifties. I asked what had brought her to Findhorn. She was reticent at first, saying,

'I'm not sure where to begin.' Rina was clearly troubled by my question. 'Well, to get away from a husband who doesn't love me for starters.'

'I'm sorry,' I said, unsure what else to say.

'Don't be. He's a jerk. It's not just that. My mother died earlier this year, that's been really hard for me.' We walked on in silence for a few more minutes.

'There's more, David, but I don't think you need to hear my tales of woe.'

'I'm happy to listen if it helps,' I said.

'Thank you,' she said, rubbing my shoulder. 'I used to be a teacher. A few months ago I was in charge of a group of girls in New Zealand on a mountaineering trip. Halfway up the mountain one of the girls slipped and fell. I've been haunted by her death ever since. I can't go back to teaching. I don't want to be with my husband. I've had the worst year of my life. You asked why I came to Findhorn? I need to find some joy in my life again.' She began to cry. I put my arms around her and hugged her. 'Thank you for listening.' she said. Tears began to well up in me too, not just because of Rina's story but also her choice of words.

A few months before my break-up, my ex and I had gone to London for a weekend together. On the Friday night we'd met an old friend of mine there and got steaming drunk with him. On the way back to our hotel my ex claimed he had come on to her and made her feel uncomfortable. I dismissed it as drunken silliness and tried changing the subject. She grew angrier at my refusal to believe her. We drunkenly bickered and shouted at each other in the street until finally she stormed off shouting:

'YOU NEVER FUCKING LISTEN!'

It was an all-too common complaint. And I had let her go, walking off in the dead of night to find her own way back to Brighton.

*

I discovered Findhorn's hot tubs that evening, hidden behind the Universal Hall and overlooking the dunes. Full of the delightful memories of hanging out in hot tubs in

Christiania, I managed to cajole the majority of my Experience Weekers to join me. It would become our ritual for the rest of the week. There was no talk of angels and elves, instead we shared jokes and listened to each other's life stories as they unfolded. Keefe, the youngest in our group, had graduated from university in Ohio that summer and been awarded a bursary to travel the world for a year studying agriculture in communities. The bursary, however, stipulated that he was not permitted to return home during that period and a longing for his family was beginning to manifest.

'Yesterday, the planet game in the ballroom made me feel what it would be like to be an island in a cold universe. I don't want to feel that ever again... that void, that emptiness...' He began to cry. Laughing through his tears he concluded, 'And I guess, I guess what I'm trying to say is... I miss my ma.'

Wim, the Dutchman, had secured his role that week as a bit of a clown. He couldn't resist butting in with jokes whenever people were talking and was always getting into trouble for 'inappropriate behaviour' such as rugby-tackling one of the focalisers in the garden when he was giving out instructions for the day. But one night, in the hot tubs, Wim quietly revealed that it was his way of dealing with the cancer that riddled his old body.

Shirley, the retired yoga teacher, spoke about Findhorn with passion.

'I'm finding this so beautiful, the care and attention with which the work is done here. I'm wondering how to take this into the real world, attunement, this sharing and nurture for each other. I mean, will we just fall back into our patterns as before?'

Carolyn, a shy woman from London, had a very different experience.

'I don't know. I just got annoyed today. I'm in the kitchen with this guy. And everything he does is just so... slow. And I want to shake him... I guess I'm used to doing things quickly. God it's frustrating.' Her feelings were written all over her face.

Carel put his arm around her and said:

'People here don't exactly get down to business, that's the Findhorn way – one man's trash is another man's treasure.'

Each evening, as the stories and personalities of our group began to unfold, I could feel tenderness for my companions beginning to grow.

*

As with Christiania, nudity was commonplace in Findhorn's hot tubs. While it didn't seem to be a big deal in these communities, being English I often get asked how I feel about getting naked with others. To be honest, I don't have any issues with it. But then I did get over my initial shyness through trial by fire. Years ago in Berlin I visited a swimming complex and, wandering about in my trunks, was about to enter the sauna when a burly female pool attendant grabbed me by the shoulder.

'If you're going in the sauna you must take off your slip.' she ordered.

'My slip?' I said, confused. The attendant pointed at

my trunks.

'Oh.' I said. A silence descended on the pool. All eyes were on me.

'TAKE THEM OFF!' bellowed the attendant. Horrified, I pulled my trunks down in front of her. 'Welcome to Germany!' she laughed, punching the air, and walked off. Ever since then, getting naked in a hot tub has been a walk in the park.

*

One afternoon I took part in an experiment. A focaliser called Daniel had just completed his teaching qualification in 'The Transformation Game' and together with my Experience Weekers Wim and Ann I had volunteered to play. The game used dice, counters and cards like Monopoly but instead of teaching players how to be fatcats, this involved the evolution of each player through different planes, moving from the physical to emotional, mental and finally the spiritual. The rules were immensely complicated. Before we could even throw a dice we had to listen for two hours. Wim kept butting in with jokes as Daniel explained the basics, but at least he didn't try and wrestle him to the ground.

I got off to a bad start, almost failing to get born. When I finally popped into the physical realm, I was already a few goes behind the others. An overwhelming impatience kicked in.

'It's the game of life. Why rush it?' said Daniel, reading my body language.

The game involved accumulating awareness, dealing with

pain, resolving conflict and helping other players deal with their problems. Sometimes one go could take up to forty-five minutes, as prolonged decision-making took place and pages of rules were read out. Each turn offered us the chance to talk about problems, relationships, blocks and feelings. Wounds were being opened up and gently sealed again. By mid-afternoon, Ann had progressed to the Mental Level, Wim was ready to transcend to the Spiritual. I remained stuck in the Physical. Several times the dice had prevented me from moving up. All I needed was to serve, give or do a charitable deed. And each time the dice let me down. By five o'clock we'd run out of time. Daniel, sensing my frustration, kindly said,

'I think we could just have time for one more go if you'd like, David?'

I did. I kept telling myself it was just a game but it seemed oddly prophetic. I really didn't want to be left on the physical plane, but the dice had other plans.

'You know what was holding you back, don't you?' said Daniel afterwards.

'No.'

'You desire with your head, not your heart. You want to perform an act of service out of desire, not out of love. The universe recognised that. It was your impatience again, getting in the way. You need to find a service in the physical world that is done with love. That will take you to the higher realm your spirit craves.'

'Such as?'

'In your case you need to find something that you enjoy

and can do with love for others. Everything we do can be love in action if done with the right intent. Curious about your block cards, don't you think though?' The two cards I'd been dealt as 'blocks' on the physical plane had been Impatience and Selfishness. I knew if my ex had been present she'd have no doubt agreed.

*

Findhorn was working its subtle magic on me. At mealtimes I was re-discovering the simple pleasure of communal meals, enjoying the wealth of conversation at the dining table with people from all over the world. Despite my apathy towards cooking and cleaning during my relationship, I found myself looking forward to clearing up after each meal when half a dozen of us crowded into the kitchen to wash up and dry and the room rang with laughter.

I was growing appreciative of attunement too. Being the kind of person who normally rushes from one task to another without stopping to think, I had struggled with this ritual before and after every activity. Now it made sense to complete a task by saying thank you and beginning the next by greeting my work colleagues and sharing the moment with them. But as Shirley had asked in the hot tub, could attunement really be something we could take back to the real world?

On the final night a party was thrown. Carel showed up with a carrier bag full of drink and we settled into the lounge at

ATTUNEMENT IN
PROGRESS,
PLEASE DO NOT
ENTER

LET YOUR MUGS, GLASSES,... ON THE TROLLEY, THANK YOU!

WITH LOVE, THE KITCHEN AND DINING ROOM CREW

Cluny Hill for a long evening of poetry, stories and jokes. An hour earlier we'd congregated outside the hotel for a group photo. Everyone had been present except Carel who'd walked off, his ever-present walking stick in hand, saying it was 'too cheesy'. Whilst we had all grown fond of Carel's mischief, he could be a stubborn sod at times. And he wasn't always easy as a roommate. As well as smoking in bed he talked in his sleep. When I say talk, I mean shout. One night he was having a party, on another he appeared to be listing different pizza toppings.

I'd begun Experience Week thinking I'd have nothing in common with my group but that evening, looking around at the faces of Ann, Wim, Carel, Rina, Shirley and the others, I felt compassion towards them. Through the simple acts of eating together, working, playing games and sharing our stories in the hot tubs, in only seven days my heart had begun to open up.

With Experience Week over I needed somewhere to stay. I moved in with Jonathan, a yoga teacher who lived in a small cottage in Findhorn village with a rocking chair, massage table, Tarot cards stuck to the walls and fairy lights around the window. I quizzed him about the 'No P, No D' written on a sticky label on his computer.

'No porn and no Debbie Harry,' he replied. 'I spend far too much time on the internet looking at both.' He then proceeded to show me his favourite Blondie clips from Youtube. 'You see that dark patch at the back of her head? She always bleached her hair herself but couldn't reach that bit so it was always black.' He smiled at me. 'Hey, fuck it, we can't be perfect all the time.'

*

While empathy had grown within me for the people at Findhorn, it had done little to transform my scepticism towards some of the tackier New Age touches around the place. There were adverts for such self-development courses as:

The Secret At The End Of Life That Will Make Death The Most Joyous Experience

How To Have A Conversation With God
How To Have A Perfect Life
Embrace Your Inner Unicorn*

These courses always seemed to be run by couples with names like *Sramdama* and *Chanabanadan*. In the adverts they're always tanned, dressed in white and sporting beatific smiles. Only after you sign up for the course do you discover that Kevin and Sandra (their real names) are going through an openly hostile divorce after Sandra copped off with some guru in Thailand, and the weekend is peppered with their daily spats and bitching. I speak here from bitter experience.

In Findhorn's store, I rolled my eyes at an advert for 'Spiritual Counselling for Pets' which featured a dewy-eyed puppy on a bed, surrounded by soft toys. The shop even sold car stickers that read: 'Miracles Happen!' or 'Never drive faster than your angels can fly!' without the necessary adjunct: 'Warning! These stickers could make other people throw up.' But when my cynicism towards such things was raging unleashed, I always had Julia to put me in my place.

Julia had been living in Findhorn since the early seventies. She was a sixty-two-year-old chain-smoking, asthma-wheezing Eastender with a penchant for colourful language and a heart full of wisdom and love. Her invitation for a 'cuppa' during my second week at Findhorn had turned into several all-night sessions fuelled by strong coffee, cigarette fumes and our mutual affliction with insomnia. We would sit around the kitchen until dawn, Julia cutting vegetables for her voluminous

*OK, I made that one up.

homemade soups, busying herself by the sink or licking her fingers and rolling great tubes of tobacco.

One evening, grumbling to her about the ubiquitous Findhorn Angel that appeared on everything from community stationery to doors and signposts, I began moaning:

'I find all this Angel of Findhorn stuff really tacky.'

Julia eyeballed me.

'It's just a fucking metaphor. Get over it.'

She filled the room with blue smoke and continued, 'Look, some of our guests come to Findhorn to talk with bleeding devas, cavort with angels and hug trees. I take that with a large pinch of salt. I'd also question the motivation of some prat wanting to share this. The point of Findhorn is to bring more compassion and awareness to people. That's why I came here. My former job was in politics. There was no possibility of working with people's souls. Here I can. That's more important than a fucking cartoon angel, right?'

After another fortnight of gardening, washing up, attending courses and finding new companions to join me in the hot tubs, the honeymoon period was up. I couldn't stay on a yoga teacher's floor indefinitely and my thirst for Blondie anecdotes had been well and truly slaked. Had I wanted to be considered for residency at Findhorn I'd have had to do another course. And another. There was 'Exploring Community Life', a twelve-week foundation programme, 'Living as a Community Guest' for a further four weeks and the six-month 'Living Educational Survival' programme. Packing all these in could take up to two years *and* cost a few thousand in the process. Besides, there's really only so much communal washing up a person needs to do in order to learn how to be more loving. For curious souls who turned up in the late sixties, Findhorn's founders would have given them a spade and a place to sleep. For the majority who now came to live as residents, savings were essential. Findhorn had earned itself a reputation as a middle- class Utopia. When I'd suggested this to Julia she retorted,

'So bloody what? Aren't the middle classes entitled to be spiritual too?'

(It was clearly an issue to some in the community. One resident quietly confided to me in the hot tub,

'What this place needs is a damned good crisis.')

I had made a real connection with some of the people at Findhorn, but could I endure the wind, the long winter months and the jets? Could I deal with its remoteness? And perhaps more importantly, could I deal with the sexlessness of the place? Even Julia had expressed doubts on this issue:

'I've had enough fucks to last a lifetime,' she wheezed, 'but I do worry that for most of the young people here their idea of dressing up is putting on their cleanest gardening clothes.'

While Findhorn *was* about as sexy as a motorway service station, it was an issue that the community was attempting to address. On my final night a couple from a German free-love community – ZEGG – had been invited to give a talk and drew quite a crowd. The speaker was a little dry ('No David, just German,' Julia corrected me) but spoke with clarity about how ZEGG was not a 'knocking shop' but a safe place to explore sex and love. I did get the impression that it was run with humourless German zeal though, especially after our poodle-haired speaker said:

'In an effort to free couples of their jealousy and possessiveness, we offer you the opportunity to watch your partner having sex with a stranger. A therapist will be at hand to talk you through any issues of jealousy and anger that may arise.'

Afterwards, a record-breaking number of us squeezed into the hot tub. I ended up squashed next to an attractive German visitor, Sabrine, who I'd met earlier in the week at a dance class. It wasn't long before the conversation moved on to love and sexuality.

'Are you going to visit ZEGG?' she asked, suggestively.

'Perhaps.'

'Can you speak German?'

'No.'

'Then you need a translator. I trust you'd welcome sharing the intimacy of the experience with me also?'

Now look, if you want the truth, straight after Findhorn I'd booked myself in for four weeks at Pluscarden Abbey, a fifteenth-century Benedictine Monastery. It was all part of my role as a seeker to explore all aspects of communal life, no matter how unappealing they first appeared. The abbey was only an hour's drive from Findhorn, which meant I had the chance to visit for an afternoon to give it the once-over. I lasted ten minutes. After buying a packet of biscuits from a silent man in the gift shop and witnessing the solemn, robed monks tiptoeing around the place, I fled. Four weeks of silence and Christian prayer, what the hell was I thinking? After months of being single I'd just had an enticing proposal from a German lady in a hot tub. What I really fancied was a spell in a free-love community.

CHAPTER 4

A Polyamorous Playground

Hearing me, some people think I am a propagandist
for sex, that I am propagating sex. If so, please tell
them they have never heard me at all.

Bhagwan Shree Rajneesh

'FUUUUUUUCK YOU, FUUUUUUCK YOUUUUUUUUU'
'AAAGGHHHHH... GOOOOO FUUUUUCK... YOUR-
SELF...AAGGHHHHH...'

I woke up and looked at the clock. It was barely eight in the
morning. Dance music thumped incessantly from the room
below me, mixed with bloodcurdling screams of abuse.

'BOOOOOLLLOOOOCKS YOUUUU CUUUUUUNT!'
'BIGGGGGG HAIRY TWAAAAAAAAAAAT!'

I groaned, rolled over, plugged my headphones in and tried
to go back to sleep. To be honest, I'd hoped that a free-love
community would be a little more peaceful than this. The lustful
thoughts I'd been cultivating at Findhorn had been trampled
underfoot since my arrival.

*

For many of us in the West, the concept of free love remains indelibly linked with the sexual revolution of the sixties: the invention of the Pill and the explosion of a new counterculture that had its epicentre in California. 'Make Love Not War' became the slogan for a new generation and in 1969 a film set in San Francisco about two polyamorous couples, *Bob & Carol & Ted & Alice*, became the fifth highest-grossing film of the year. It may be apocryphal that, as a consequence, a craze for cocktail parties ending with 'car keys in the bowl' swept through suburbia, but the Swinging Sixties was undoubtedly a promiscuous decade.

It was also an era that saw an explosion of intentional communities that dabbled with free love and nudity, especially in the US. By the late sixties, weary of battles with the authorities, many of California's counterculture fled San Francisco and LA to create their own utopias outside of society. Thousands moved to the wilderness of California and New Mexico to establish micro-communes with small groups of friends sharing a farm or ranch. While polyamory was not uncommon, only a very small number developed into free love communes that were open to the public. The most famous was Hog Farm in California, established by a peace activist called Wavy Gravy (or Hugh to his mum), inviting visitors to take a more open approach to sexual relationships. While a liberal attitude to sex prevails at Hog Farm today, it has gradually shifted its attention from free love and drug culture to environmental concerns. After all, when AIDS cast its shadow in the eighties, promiscuity started to be viewed as a way of life that was more reckless than liberating. For some of today's intentional communities, an assumption that residents are, by nature, promiscuous, has become an outdated stereotype. For others, it is still a lifestyle to be experimented with or, in the case of Findhorn at least, a hot topic of conversation. Modern-day polyamorous communities such as Tamera in Portugal and ZEGG in Berlin offer a more therapeutic approach to free love, with discussions and workshops. As learned from ZEGG's poodle-haired representative at Findhorn, there is now a great deal of psychological work on 'negative' emotions around sex, such as the jealousy and possessiveness that can arise when sharing partners. On the thorny issue of perms for men however, the Germans still have much to learn.

While promiscuity was a taboo before the sixties, a purer idea of 'free love' – the rejection of the laws of marriage – was not uncommon in earlier experimental communities. Between the 1840s and 1930s many of these communities existed in Europe, offering a heady mix of communism, naturism, anarchy and free love. One such place was La Maison de Poetes in the Pyrenees, set up by an adventuress called Léonore Labilliére. In the book *Eroticism in Religion*, Labilliére was quoted as saying, 'Free love ought not to mean promiscuity, but merely a license to find one's true partner by a process of experimentation.' Other communities experimenting with sexuality and naturism have appeared in more surprising places, such as Oneida, based in upstate New York during the mid-1800s.

At a time in the US's history when most of the religious white settlers were still in the throes of Puritanism, Oneida combined Christian morality with feminism and compulsory inter-marital relationships. It was hugely radical. At Oneida all members were considered married to each other. Women over fourteen were considered equal to men and given freedom in their lifestyle choices and jobs. To help avoid teenage pregnancies, younger men were encouraged to have sex with post-menopausal women until they had mastered the art of ejaculation control. Oneida lasted over forty years before folding and, bizarrely, re-inventing itself as a manufacturing company making top-quality knives and forks. Ironically, its former location is now a hotspot for monogamous wedding ceremonies.

A year before my travels, my friend Susan had packed her bags to go and live with a free-love community in Switzerland, set up by a well-toned Brazilian who fancied himself as a reincarnation of Leonardo Da Vinci. Members practised tantric sex with each other and graded each other's performances the following morning in front of the rest of the community. They also had a strict rule that no one bigger than a size 14 could be part of the group, but had made an exception for Susan after she kicked up a fuss. I decided to strike it off my list of potential places to visit, it sounded awful. Susan still lives in Switzerland, though her love affair with the community was short-lived after an incident involving a cross-dressing Finn, some strong weed, a packet of 'Space Dust' (a seventies confectionery that fizzed in your mouth), Susan's ear and a trip to the hospital. I know it's irritating not to share the full story but I'm sworn to secrecy. To be honest, she'll kill me for what I've written already.

A reminder that the sexual mores of the West are but one part of the story is exemplified by the people of the Trobriand Islands in the West Pacific. These islanders take a very liberal approach to fornication. For centuries, premarital sex has been widespread and practised simply for fun. Trobriands change partners often in the belief that women are just as desiring of sex as the men. Rather than heavy petting as fore-play however, they prefer to scratch. If a male can withstand the pain from an interested party they will have sex. All islanders bear visible scars from sexual activity. While sex before marriage is acceptable, eating together is not. Couples may only dine together once married and if, after a year, the woman is unhappy with her husband, she will divorce him, taking her best dinner plates with her.

Trobriand children enjoy total freedom and independence. From as early as five they create their own communities, seeing their parents during the day and hanging out with their peers in the evening. If a decision to do something is made in opposition to the adults or even the leader of the island, the children have the last say. Relations between older men and younger girls are frowned upon, not as being morally wrong but rather, according to one islander, 'improper and silly.'

Curiously, the islanders do not equate sex with conception. They believe instead that the spirits of dead ancestors are responsible for fertility. While having healthy sexual appetites, birth rates are relatively low, which can be explained by a heavy yam diet that acts as a mild contraceptive. The Trobriand Islands demonstrate that a society free of sexual hang-ups is still possible in the twenty-first century providing, of course, that you don't understand how babies are really made.

As for contemporary communities exploring alternative sexual lifestyles, the heavyweight contenders can be whittled down to just a handful, which include the likes of ZEGG and Tamera. The daddy of them all, however, is Pune (pronounced *poo-na*), set up in India in the seventies by Bhagwan Shree Rajneesh (or Osho as he was later known). From the onset, Pune seemed tailor-made for libidinous westerners to fully express their desires. Having promised myself I would stay off the hippy trail in India, I found an Osho community in England instead, but so far it was nothing like I had imagined a free-love community to be.

The community was based in a large old Edwardian house, less grand than Cluny Hill Hotel but not without its charm. In the communal area by the front door sat four northerners amid a litter of beer cans and ashtrays. They were immersed in an animated conversation until they spotted me by the door with my bags. One of them got up, showed me upstairs to my dorm, waved vaguely down the corridor and said, 'You'll find the showers and stuff down there,' and left me to it. I clearly wasn't going to get a guided tour or even a proper welcome. In my dorm, a man sat on another bed looking dejected. John had left Leeds in search of a new way of life and had been living at the community for a few weeks. He asked if I wanted to watch a film.

'What have you got?' I asked.

'Every film that was made last year.'

'Really?' He opened a bag next to his bed. Inside were hundreds of DVDs in flat plastic wallets.

'I took last year off so I thought I'd catch up on my cinema. One in the morning, one in the afternoon, one in the evening. A thousand in a year.'

'Christ, well, what would you recommend?'

'Dunno, to be honest they're all a bit crap,' he muttered. I could see it would be laugh-a-minute with this guy. After unpacking in silence I thought I'd rather try my luck with the men downstairs.

The quartet grunted as I sat down. I hoped I might be offered a drink in the spirit of camaraderie but instead they continued with their conversation. As if on cue, the chosen subject was Osho.

'He was the most enlightened person on the fucking planet,' one of them was arguing.

'Enlightened? Don't be fucking soft. You don't know shit about enlightenment. When you're enlightened you *leave* the fucking planet. Everyone knows that. Osho hadn't left the planet. He was driving round it in a sodding Rolls Royce. He was a dude, man.'

'A "dude"? What is this? Bill and Ted? He was a fucking rebel,' another interjected.

'Bollocks! He was a fucking comedian. Listen, when they kicked him out of the States he was going round the world in his private jet trying to find somewhere to stay. And when Greece finally let him in, do you know what he did?'

There was a round of 'hmm's' and ferocious nodding.

'He did a press conference, stood up and said, "Father, son and holy ghost? Where's the women? Sounds like a pretty gay religion you've got going on here!"' There was a self-satisfied pause and slurping of beer.

'Ever go to Pune?' I asked. They turned and stared, having forgotten I was there.

'Sure, mate,' one of them said, 'it's pretty tame now compared to what it was. I went in the seventies. God it was wild at the beginning. Women were getting raped, people were physically fighting each other, legs were getting broken.' There were a few sniggers.

'Er, was that a good thing?'

'No 'course not, but they were just finding their feet, weren't they?'

'Hey, not if their legs were broken they weren't,' another one laughed.

I had arrived at the commune late at night, after a tortuously long two-day drive from Scotland. As I'd reached the Scottish border on the first day of the drive, I'd picked up a couple of young hitchhikers from Eastern Europe who had been working at a farm in Scotland and now, by coincidence, were travelling to my old home town of Doncaster, looking for work. I was heading to Doncaster too, planning a night at my parents' house to break up the seventeen-hour journey. My passengers were quiet for most of the journey and we spent much of the time listening to the radio. On Radio 4's *Desert Island Discs* that day was Simon Cowell, a man who has done much to validate karaoke as a second-rate artform. As he discussed his musical choices, wealth and history, the presenter suddenly butted in and said,

'But are you *happy*, Simon?'

He thought about it for a moment then said:

'I can never be happy knowing there are other people out there more successful than me.'

As I approached my companions' desired drop-off point, by the ASDA roundabout near the centre of Doncaster, I heard mutterings from them about a tent.

'Are you camping tonight?' I asked, a little surprised.

'Oh yes.'

'But there's no campsite in Doncaster,' I said.

'We'll find somewhere.'

'Really, you won't. I know this town, I grew up here. There's no campsite for miles. You can't just camp by a roundabout. Come and stay with my folks,' I said, knowing my mother would have a heart attack at the idea of strangers staying under her roof.

'No, we're happy to camp where we're dropped off. It's what we always do.'

'Don't the police hassle you?'

'It's no big deal,' they giggled. 'They're nice. They usually let us stay until the morning.'

It was getting dark as I dropped them near ASDA and

watched them begin to unpack their tent in my rear-view mirror. I admired their naivety and inherent sense of joy, a welcome reminder that wealth and fame are far from being prerequisites for happiness.

Before leaving Findhorn the previous morning, I'd checked out directions on the Osho community's website. It had shown pictures of men and women hugging, kissing and laughing. Not a gaggle of pissed Northerners.*

I left the Four Yorkshiremen to it, effing and blinding their way through a discourse on metaphysics and gurus and wandered back to the dorm to listen to a recording of Osho I had downloaded. His serpentine voice lulled me to sleep. 'You are not my followerssssssssss, you are ssssssimply my friendssssssssssssss...'

The first day passed quietly with work duties and meals. I cleaned the kitchen, hoovered the stairs and wiped surfaces as requested. The house and grounds were quiet. Only a couple of dozen people appeared to be living in the community full time. Mealtimes were strangely sober. Nobody seemed interested in my presence there and as they weren't forthcoming with information about themselves or the community when asked, I sensed they preferred their privacy. After twenty-four hours I wondered what I was doing there. Rather than being the polyamorous playground I had heard about, it felt more like a halfway home for those who'd lost their way or needed a place to recharge their batteries. I waited for the weekend

---

*I have nothing against Northerners by the way; quite the opposite. I was raised in Doncaster on pies, drizzle and sarcasm and you can't get more typically Northern than that.

to come and drifted around the building reading Osho's books and watching videos about him in the library, his Joan Collins shoulder pads and aviator shades getting bigger as the documentaries moved from the seventies to the eighties. I was missing the company of Carel, Julia, Wim, Ann, Keefe and my other Experience Weekers from Findhorn. And, inevitably, my thoughts drifted back to my ex.

That morning I had received a devastating email. Mere months after our break-up, my ex had suddenly announced her engagement to Dougal and was emigrating to Australia. I'd been secretly nursing hopes of a reunion after returning home as the newly-improved former boyfriend who she was still secretly in love with. If that wasn't enough to depress the hell out of me, she concluded by writing that she and Dougal were 'now planning on living a totally new and more fulfilling way of life in Australia'. What did that mean? What could Australia offer apart from BBQs, venomous creepy crawlies and Crocodile Dundee? It was time to try and throw off all emotional ties to my ex through the carnal delights of a free-love community.

Like Findhorn, the community made a living by running courses with titles like: 'Find Your Bliss' and 'Dying to Live'. They ran throughout the year, bringing a fresh influx of people at weekends. It was then that the place really came alive, with New Age partygoers, shy men and women and curious first-timers. Asking a group over breakfast one morning about Osho and his teachings, I found to my surprise that none of them seemed to know much about him.

'He was a love guru, that's all I know,' one woman said.

'When I was here last year, two girls asked for their money back. They'd heard orgies were taking place and wanted to leave. They got quite hysterical about it,' another woman said.

'Were there?' I asked.

'Wouldn't surprise me,' a red-faced man interjected with weary cynicism. I was confused. I honestly thought those visiting would be open-minded to the idea of free love.

'So why are you here?' I asked him.

'I just want to dance myself into exhaustion,' he replied, and his friends nodded in agreement.

'What about you then?' he asked, 'why are you here?'

'I came out of a relationship recently. I'm on a journey... in search of Utopia,' came my stock reply.

'Don't you know that Utopia is here?' one of the women said, pointing to her heart.

'And you're hoping to get laid as well, I imagine?' said the cynical red-faced man.

'Well, yes,' I said, feeling my cheeks flush red at the public confession.

Judging by the reactions of some of those around me I might as well have said that I liked biting the ears off kittens.

Later that morning, my mealtime companions got their wish as we took part in a 'Power Dance' in the main hall. For over two hours we threw ourselves around to Tina Turner and Status Quo, with our dance guide yelling: 'Come on, whoo yeah! Let's get some love and energy in the room. Clap your hands! Punch the air!' The terrible music and the air-punching were too much for me. I felt like an interloper at a motivational weekend for clapped-out businessmen.

In the afternoon we were invited to take part in the 'big one'; the notorious three-hour AUM meditation, which had woken me with such a start on my first morning at the community with all the bloodcurdling screams.

'This is for releasing trapped emotion, the chance for a life-changing experience,' said one of the Four Yorkshiremen.

'If you start to disengage, don't allow it to happen. Get angry with yourself. Say "no, fucker, I won't let you win".'

Fifty of us wandered around the room as the music warmed up then, on cue, the abuse began. For a full ten minutes I yelled 'AAAAAAGGGGHHHHHHHH, FUCK YOU, FUCKING FUCK OFF. FUCK YOUUUUUUUU AND YOUR BIG HAIRY BOLLOCKSSSSSSSSSSSS' into the face of some poor man who looked like he was about to cry. He was meant to be yelling abuse back at me but the best he could muster was 'Shove off, you tosser.' This was followed by a further ten minutes in which we asked someone's forgiveness. I sought out my abused companion to redress the balance but he'd teamed up with someone else. After this, in further ten-minute sections, we were asked to laugh, cry, clown around like kids, shake and do a 'sexy dance'. Finally we were asked to 'express some intimacy with a stranger'. The Four Yorkshiremen made straight for the new blood in the room and began dry humping on the floor. Following suit, other couplings were made until all the women in the room were taken. An excess of men remained, myself included. We wandered around looking lost, pretending not to notice each other for fear we'd have to dry hump each other too. By teatime it was over. We punched the air in jubilation. My throat was torn to pieces from all the yelling. I had enjoyed taking part in such an intense experience; it challenged my English reserve. And I can't deny that the AUM meditation *did* get my emotions stirred up. But then, on reflection, so does my mother.

*

Where Findhorn's founders had been the Compo, Foggy and Clegg of the spiritual movement (gender not withstanding), Osho was its Marlon Brando: a man who played the bad-boy guru to perfection. A former philosophy professor, Osho started travelling around India in the late sixties giving lectures.

'Because it is condemned, sex has become an obsession, a disease,' he declared. 'Organised religion has spent so long making a taboo out of sex that we have become obsessed with it. The solution is to educate our children properly about sex and nudity and allow them to explore it without condemnation and judgement. After all, is not life an infinitely non-ending process of procreation?' By talking openly about sex and attacking organised religion, Osho made himself notorious from the offset and quickly gained a following. His first community, Pune, offered everything for the Western spiritual tourist: group therapy, daily meditations, ninety-minute lectures and an air of permissiveness. By the eighties, Osho needed somewhere bigger but clashes with the Indian authorities meant that the group were denied access to land. Osho's lectures had also started to raise a few eyebrows. His philosophical diatribes had been replaced with smutty and sometimes racist jokes.

The community relocated to Oregon where Osho set up Rajneeshpura, an intentional community of twenty thousand followers, around which Osho would take daily drives in one of his ninety-six Rolls-Royces. Rajneeshpura was dogged with problems from the start and spats with the locals grew increasingly unpleasant. By 1983, the community desperately wanted to get its own mayor elected in an upcoming local election. To keep the opposition at bay, Osho's secretary Sheela contaminated salad bars and coffee creamers with salmonella in over ten different restaurants on the day of the election. Over four hundred people were poisoned, many of them hospitalised. It remains to this day the largest case of chemical warfare against the American people. Osho was incarcerated for two weeks and finally returned to Pune where he died at the age of fifty-eight, claiming he had been poisoned with a drug called thallium whilst imprisoned in the US. It seemed unlikely, as one of the side-effects of thallium is baldness: Osho died with a full head of hair.

Having started a spiritual path as a teacher condemning false gurus, Osho ended up the most decadent of them all. By the eighties he had badmouthed Gandhi and Mother Theresa, described Jesus as 'plain crazy' and publicly called for the assassination of Mikhail Gorbachev. Some of his supporters argued that Osho's 'mental decline' was down to health problems. ME, back pain, Stage 2 diabetes and asthma, his followers claimed, had led to his addiction to nitrous oxide and Valium, which turned him a bit odd.

Despite the notoriety and self-aggrandisement, in his early years Osho wrote a number of profound books on the themes of love, sex and self-awareness. In *Sex and Superconsciousness* he argues that the reason we're all so hung up on sex in the West is that at the moment of orgasm we experience, for a very brief period, a sense of egolessness and timelessness. Put another way – a glimpse of God. Rather than expending huge amounts of our time and energy searching for the next fleeting moment of bliss, this sexual energy can become pure love through particular meditative and sexual practices. 'The evolution of love,' Osho wrote, 'is nothing but transformed sexual energy.' In the early days, the great sex guru hadn't been arguing for more sex, but a greater awareness during the act of lovemaking. Despite Osho's claim that his message was misunderstood, his communities continue to be associated with promiscuity. And to get things rolling on this front, ours had organised a fancy dress party and disco.

Never one to turn down the chance to dress up in a ridiculous costume, I paid a visit to the fancy-dress room late one afternoon and found a black grey wig and furry Russian hat. It gave me an idea for a costume. I tied the wig around my chin, donned a white robe and the hat and transformed myself into Osho. That evening, nodding sagely at my fellow visitors, I strolled around giving blessings and words of wisdom, rolling my words as I'd heard Osho do, 'Never eat yellow sssssssssssssnow.'

The Four Yorkshiremen scowled their disapproval, but they had their own agenda that night. By nine, they had their shirts off and were strutting around like peacocks in the main hall as the clanging sounds of Erasure echoed through the building. The place began to fill with people dancing and drinking. I noticed the red-faced man in one corner, kissing and fondling a young woman. I knew he'd been economical with the truth about just coming to the Osho community to dance – he was hoping to get laid like the rest of us. More couples began to pair off in the gloom. It was a far cry from the stories I'd heard of Pune where naked men and women would wander around offering tantric massages and orgy rooms would be full of great writhing bodies. Instead, here we were at a glorified school disco, still too ashamed to articulate our desires without alcohol, fancy dress and Huey Lewis and the News. But I won't deny it, I had my fun that night too. Over the previous few days I'd made friends with a woman called Jo and now we too were flirting on the dance floor. Later we retired to her campervan. She insisted I keep the beard on for the night. We made a great double act: an Osho impersonator and an NLP practitioner from Croydon. By the next day however, my thoughts returned to my ex.

It dawned on me later why I had felt so unwelcome that first day at the community: I was potential competition to the Four Yorkshiremen. One of them even admitted as much in an afternoon encounter group when he complained of having commitment issues and saw the community as a way of avoiding this whilst still pursuing his carnal desires. I wondered how different my experience might have been if the community had been run by women.

While it all seemed harmless enough, there was one thing about the place that *had* bothered me. Lurking in the shadows during the Saturday night fancy-dress parties were the lonely ones: timid souls who'd come to the community in the hope of a bit of intimacy. Instead, they had to watch the more confident or lucky among us getting amorous. They came feeling lonely and left the same way. I felt for them. Findhorn and Christiania had seemed like communities that looked out for people. If this really was a loving community, as it claimed to be, shouldn't someone have been nurturing these people too?

To be fair, the Osho community wasn't a fully-fledged free-love community and neither did it present itself as such. I needed to visit ZEGG for the full experience but, to be honest, I didn't have the heart. As a lifestyle choice, polyamory has never held much sway for me. Success stories amongst friends in open relationships were as rare as hen's teeth, while disastrous experiments with threesomes were all too commonplace. Despite other shortcomings in my relationship with my ex, I had never strayed. But then I've never been in a sexless relationship. I've seen friends, both male and female, almost at their wits' end at the loss of sexual intimacy with their partners. I've known others have illicit affairs and visit prostitutes. Some, unwilling to cheat on their partners, have taken to extreme sports and even obsessive cake-baking to take their minds off it. One friend however, in talking it over openly with her husband, found him compliant with her discreetly taking a lover. When her husband is away, her lover parks his van round the corner and sends her a text. After some carnal passion in the back of the van she goes home again.

'I've got everything I need,' she confided in me, 'a husband I love and a terrific sex life. But I feel so guilty.'

Despite obsessing about sex, most of us still seem ashamed to discuss or deal with our sexual hang-ups in an open, honest way, even, as I discovered, in a supposedly permissive community. I remembered how embarrassed I had felt at being forced to admit that I'd been hoping to 'get laid' at the Osho community. Our newspapers don't help matters either. Almost every day our prurient tabloids are filled with sex scandals, three-in-a-bed romps and the exposé of another celebrity caught receiving a blowjob in a lay-by. While we're supposed to feel moral outrage, the real scandal is the very fact that these papers are still filled with titillating pictures and bare-breasted 'dollybirds' as out-dated as a Benny Hill sketch.

But while the media's obsession with sex and the macho shenanigans at the Osho community all felt a bit tired and tawdry, they weren't the only aspect of sexuality I encountered during my research. One sex community uniquely challenged the modern utopian principles of equality, freedom and bliss. This was the Other World Kingdom, a great fantasy playground set up by a mysterious benefactor for people to explore and live out their singular kinky fantasies in a community controlled entirely by women.

In his book *Rituals of Love*, the social anthropologist Ted Polhemus argues that the sexual revolution of the sixties made
casual sex easier but in doing so cast out important rituals
of courtship and the frisson of seduction. Once there was a
time when a man and woman would court over a number of
months, sometimes years, with words, love letters and a walk
in the park. The most intimate encounter they were likely to
have before marriage would be a kiss on the cheek. The sexual
tension must have been electric. Nowadays things are very
different. We have commodified sex. It has become like junk
food to many of us, a quick but unsatisfying fix; a drunken
conversation at a nightclub, a quickie round the back of the
car park, curry and chips and the bus home. We may be more
obsessed with sex but rather than approaching it as a banquet
we treat it like a Pot Noodle. In direct opposition to this,
Polhemus argues, the world of fetishism has evolved, with its
complex rituals, shiny clothes, role-play and impractical foot-
wear. It is a lifestyle that eschews freedom in favour of sub-
mission and power; it blurs the boundaries between pain and
pleasure and, in some cases, involves the total surrender of
control to another.

I first heard about the Other World Kingdom through an
article that a friend, Mark, had written for a kinky lifestyle
magazine, *Skin Two*. While Mark's visit (and article) had
been brief, my curiosity had been piqued by his descriptions
of a castle complex in the heart of the Czech Republic run by
dominant women, for whom men were their servants.

'It's a Disneyland for perverts, there's nothing else like it on the planet,' Mark said, 'though the food is appalling.'

Set in the buildings and grounds of a sixteenth-century castle, the Other World Kingdom boasted its own flag, currency (the Dom) and a state hymn that sounded like Russ Abbott's 'Atmosphere' played on a tuba. It described itself as an gynarchy, with its own Queen Patricia and her team of sublime ladies, a fantastic sexualised human hive with its own kinky Queen Bee. Here men were the inferior class, subject to slavery, serfdom, torture, imprisonment without a fair trial and on occasion, being dressed as a giant spider and whipped. The only major gaff seemed to be in calling itself a kingdom. And if a kinky Utopia should require a sense of purpose, Mark showed me their ambitious manifesto on the website:

> **The goal of the Other World Kingdom is to get as many male creatures under the unlimited rule of Superior Women on as much territory as possible. Gradual realization of this goal will mean the introduction of an Absolute Matriarchy – the only righteous social order.**

It brought to mind *The Worm That Turned*, a weekly serialised comedy story from the eighties by the Two Ronnies, depicting a world where men had been reduced to doing menial house-work and wearing aprons while the ladies swanned around in black PVC and knee-high boots, ruling with an iron fist. It was clearly the erotic fantasy of one of the Ronnies, and my money is on the little one, Corbett. Like *The Worm That Turned*, the

Other World Kingdom was not without humour, as its taxation system (also on the website) showed:

> The subordinate class (i.e. men) are required to pay manhood tax during their visit. This is calculated by multiplying the length of the erect penis in centimetres by the coefficient 4. If the penis is incapable of achieving lift-off, the coefficient increases to 12. Exceptions are made for any subordinate class who is the father of 3 daughters and no sons, is on state benefits, or has no penis.

A few months later, I found another article about the Other World Kingdom in *Skin Two*, written by an adventurous journalist who had spent twenty-four hours there. In describing her experience, she wrote:

'The first day began with a short ceremony during which the State Flag was raised, the State Hymn was sung and the ladies participated in a symbolic punishment of the male race for all the crimes perpetrated by them on women through the ages.' Later, she attended 'a civil court at which slaves were tried for infractions to the rules by Lady Mona, who metered out carefully constructed corrective sentences.'

I learned too that, with a permanent entourage of thirty or so 'sublime ladies', the Other World Kingdom offered the chance for men to sign themselves up for short-term and even permanent residency, leaving behind their old lives in favour of subservience to womankind.

'One man,' the article related, 'spent a whole month living as a horse, sleeping on straw in the stables every night, and not being allowed to interact with anyone as a human being during the whole of that time.'

In planning my year away, I had ummed and ahhed about visiting the Other World Kingdom. I still couldn't decide if it truly qualified as a real community or whether it was simply a glorified (if unique) sex resort for the fetish crowd. But after my experiences at the Osho community, all such doubts evaporated. Following an endless list of questions fired over the phone to the Other World Kingdom's 'receptionist' (a grumpy-sounding Eastern European man) I decided to book my flight to the Czech Republic. As a seeker with a taste for the exotic, the chance to visit a kinky community, far from the world of wind chimes, school discos, alpha males and half-baked New Age Philosophy, was too fantastic to miss.

*

The tiny hamlet of Cerná in the Czech countryside seemed an unlikely home for an S&M kingdom. There was a decrepit farm, a few houses, an old lady feeding the ducks by a pond and a handful of kids idling about in the trees. Rather preposterously, in the centre of this scene of pastoral bliss stood the high walls of the Other World Kingdom, an impenetrable fortress, its central tower pointing towards the sky from which it appeared to have fallen.

I parked outside and banged on the hefty old oak door. After several minutes a sad-faced man in a dog collar opened the little shutter, his melancholic visage filling the small square hatch. 'Come.' A great wooden bolt was released and to complete the full gothic setting an immense hardwood door creaked its way into action.

I had been granted exclusive permission to visit the Other World Kingdom as a 'visitor'. 'Look don't touch,' had been the instruction of the surly male receptionist on the phone. While spared the humiliation of being measured for manhood tax, I had also been charged a heavy fee to visit for a few days.

After signing in and exchanging my Euros for Doms, I was set free to explore. I was surprised at what lay beyond the walls. With the warmth of the sun, the trees in blossom and an array of impressive white-painted buildings, the Other World Kingdom looked like a well-groomed stately home. The vast, serene and empty grounds seemed a far cry from the shadowy images I'd seen online – the forbidding tower, dank dungeons

and grumpy-looking dominatrixes whipping great red welts across the backsides of hairy, naked men.

I wandered into the bar (empty), checked the temperature of the water in the indoor swimming pool (cold), and had a nose at the other bedrooms (also empty). Up one set of stairs I found a large, dark nightclub strewn with limp balloons, full ashtrays and dusty pint glasses still filled with flat, stale beer, its guests seemingly whisked away by some unforeseen calamity. It was like *Westworld*. Where was everybody? As I journeyed from building to building, I did occasionally catch a glimpse of a short fat Japanese man in a 'State Slave' t-shirt, skulking in the shadows, but whenever I approached he slipped away.

What the Other World Kingdom lacked by way of humans, it more than made up for in dead flies. There were thousands of them, as if a great plague had blown through the building, taken one look at all the kinky equipment and dropped dead out of sheer embarrassment.

The sad-faced man in the dog collar seemed to be in charge of the cooking, cleaning and general maintenance of the Other World Kingdom. He also seemed to spend much of his time in the bar, glued to the Czech equivalent of *Pop Idol*. I wandered in to get a drink. There were flies all over the bar. The sad-faced man appeared to be eating what looked like tripe and cornflakes. Before leaving, I'd read on a forum that the worst torture at the Other World Kingdom was the food, so had filled my suitcase with Pot Noodles, which turned out to be lifesavers.

'Glass of white wine please,' I said. The sad-faced man

pointed at the only two bottles behind the bar: Cinzano and Malibu.

As I stood around sipping the first of many Malibus that night, I noticed that the Japanese man had stepped into the back of the bar and was staring at me. For the first and only time during my visit, the sad-faced man engaged me in conversation.

'Don't worry about Frank,' he said, in his melancholic, Eastern European accent, 'he's been terribly unhappy since the ladies have left.'

The same sinking feeling that had come over me when I'd first stepped into Christiania returned.

'Are you saying they're *not* coming back?'

'Yah. The queen fell out with sublime ladies a few weeks ago. They wanted pay rise. She refused. There was enormous cat fight.' He clicked his fingers, 'Pffft. Everybody go.' Engaging me with a knowing look, he rolled his eyes. 'You know what women can be like'.

'So what's Frank still doing here?'

'He loves the place. He doesn't want to leave. Sometimes he gets to be an extra when people come to make the porn. Trouble is, Frank's spent so much of his life on all fours that his knees are totally fucked. He's not much use any more. He cannot kneel down. They just have him standing in the background. It is pity.'

I could understand now why I'd been permitted to visit. I'd paid full price to visit an empty amusement park. The joke was on me. The Other World Kingdom, I would later discover, was up for sale. After less than fifteen years, the kinky bubble had burst.

I moped around the next day, eating Pot Noodles and exploring more of the grounds. The Other World Kingdom's coat of arms, a pair of handcuffs and a whip, were to be found on everything from the packaging on bars of soap to the beermats. I found the human kennels and stables where I'd read that men had once lived as dogs and horses. In another building was a vast collection of S&M ephemera and a great library of kinky literature. In the queen's residence stood a throne with fat metal rings at its base for attaching chained slaves. Nearby, her sedan chair stood at the ready. Underneath her palace were the dungeons: rows of single windowless prison cells, too small to lie down in, each with a chain attached to the wall and a metal bowl. I noticed with some relief that each prison was fitted with a bright red 'panic button'.

While it was the sobriety and sexlessness of the monastery in Scotland that kept me from experimenting with that ascetic lifestyle, I couldn't help noticing comparisons between The Other World Kingdom and these old Christian communes. Both were places of worship, and both had used solitary confinement and flagellation as a means to explore altered states of consciousness. Was it too much of a stretch of the imagination to see the Other World Kingdom as a kind of monastic order where men venerated women as goddesses (albeit role-playing goddesses squeaking around in PVC)?

At the far end of the grounds was a sports arena: a dark barn full of traps and racing equipment where the Sublime Ladies had raced their slaves. It was here that every summer the Other World Kingdom once hosted the Slave Olympics, a kinky *It's a Knockout* attracting mistresses and slaves from all over the world to indulge in some top-class entertainment. Games had ranged from potentially life-threatening to the downright silly, including the 'Largest Number of Ladies Standing Together With Their Full Weight on One Male Creature Competition', 'Face-slapping Billiards', the 'Pushing Lady's High Heel Shoe fifty metres with Slave-Nose Event' and the 'Highest Pain Tolerance Award'. I read somewhere that this last award was held by State Slave Brynn, who endured an impressive three hours and twelve minutes of whipping one summer. I wonder where they buried him?

That evening, to my surprise, a couple turned up. In the main lounge area near my room, a woman dressed in leather was sitting on a large chair below a notice for 'ladies shoeshine'. A man in a pair of leather trousers and Freddie Krueger jumper knelt polishing her boots. I averted my eyes from the scene, expecting them to want to be left alone in their ritual, so was surprised when they both lunged towards me with big smiles.

'It is our fifth visit,' Frans from Austria explained, 'something we treat ourselves to every year.' He wrapped Claudia's hand in his, with the look of a man still hopelessly in love. I later learned that they had been married for over twenty years.

'We love it here. So pretty,' Claudia said, 'but the food is terrible. We have learned to bring our own. You will join us for picnic?'

Glad to escape another Bombay Bad Boy, I joined them in one of the main halls. Surrounding us were cages, kennels, whips and torture devices. Claudia laid a picnic blanket on the floor filled with a variety of fine cheeses, wine, salad and crusty bread. We indulged in small talk until, inevitably, the pair asked what had brought me to the Other World Kingdom. I explained about my journey to explore Utopia.

'You know a *genuine* Utopia?' Frans asked. 'Sub-space. When you lose yourself completely in S&M roleplay. Detach from all reality. The ego surrenders and there's no sense of time or space. That's Utopia surely?'

Claudia nodded her approval.

Frans' choice of words echoed the sentiments of something I'd read by Osho only the previous week. He had described states of deep meditation and techniques for awakening the consciousness that took a person to a place of 'no ego, time or space'. From the intimacy and focus I'd observed (discreetly) between Frans and Claudia when playing out their roles, they were as much 'in the zone' as any yoga or meditation practice. And if orgasm is indeed a brief experience of the divine, as Osho believed, do S&M rituals offer a more prolonged taste of bliss? A picnic rather than a Pot Noodle?

Being placed in solitary confinement in a cold prison cell at the Other World Kingdom was someone's idea of Utopia. It defies our inherent sense of what it is to be free. As a lifestyle, S&M flies in the face of every utopian ideal of the twenty-first century. A gay friend of mine once described the fetish world as, 'sex for people who need counselling', but then *he* likes having a butt plug carved out of ginger root stuck up his arse, so who are we to judge? And besides, it wasn't that long ago in the UK that we used to view homosexuality as deviant and unnatural. Could we not instead see S&M as part of our sexual evolution: an antidote to the 'quick fix', combining ritual and costume, blurring the lines between traditional gender roles, between pleasure and pain?

Whether the Other World Kingdom ever really functioned as a proper gynarchy or was simply a millionaire's lavish fantasy remained a mystery. For me, its uniqueness lay in the incredible detail that had been applied to keep the fantasy as real as possible. The *Skin Two* journalist had concluded her article by saying, 'I don't really care who put up the money to create it... I'm just glad that this leather Neverland really does exist.' But the reality of maintaining the Other World Kingdom had clearly been too much for its creators. It brought to mind an adage often given as a warning to those who dream about the romance of owning their own boat but overlook the reality of its upkeep: 'the two happiest days of a boat owner's life are the day they buy it, and the day they sell it.'

For those of us whose fantasy world involves a cast of hundreds, singing plants and a giant underground temple, Utopia is best left in the realms of our imagination. Otherwise – even with money and the best will in the world – we may find Utopia a bit too much like hard work. Unless, that is, we happen to possess the work ethic and vision of a community that calls itself Damanhur.

CHAPTER 5

In Search of a Man Called Gorilla Eucalyptus

In the summer of 1978, a small community of Italians calling themselves 'Damanhur' bought an area of land in the foothills of the Alps near Turin and began digging in secret at night. Their leader, a man called Oberto Airaudi (or Falco, to his followers) instructed them to build a temple 'the like of which has not been seen for thousands of years'. Within half a year a modest-sized chamber was completed. They celebrated by holding a small marriage ceremony there.

For the next thirteen years, in an operation that would have made the building of the Tom, Dick and Harry tunnels in *The Great Escape* seem like child's play, two million buckets of rock, earth and clay were removed from the mountain. By 1991, nine separate temples had been completed, boasting marble floors, stained-glass ceilings, mosaics, carved columns, statues and covering an area equivalent in size to St Paul's Cathedral.

The Damanhurians were careful to cover their tracks. The house that sheltered the temples' entrance was the perfect cover: anyone who saw the trucks going up and down the mountain would presume they were doing structural work to the building. Even if someone had chanced upon the entrance to the temple, they wouldn't have got far: each chamber was hidden by secret solid stone doors that only revealed their secret to the 'initiated' (or anyone who knew where the switch was hidden). Besides, would the locals really have believed that the Eighth Wonder of the World had quietly been built in the Piedmont Mountains in secret, right under their noses?

As the community of Damanhur grew from thirty-odd to several hundred, so did hostility from the authorities. In 1991, the Vatican declared Turin to be a hotbed for black magic and cults. While there probably *were* a handful of depressed teenagers listening to doom metal and daubing graffiti on the local church, it was Damanhur – because of its size and presence – that really attracted the attention of the Catholic hardliners. A smear campaign began, with one cardinal describing the Damanhurians as 'a cult of idolaters, indulging in orgies, adultery, drunkenness and witchcraft'.

Later that year, on October 8th at 6am, Damanhur's residents awoke to find the police and army swarming all over their property. There were sniffer dogs, helicopters, cameras and more than two hundred officers armed with pistols and machine guns. The police were primed for 'a potentially dangerous situation'. This was a raid bigger than anything the Mafia had experienced. But if the cops were expecting to find any evidence of *Wicker Man*-style sacrifices and stews made from newborn babies, they were disappointed. As one of Damanhur's founders was later proud of pointing out, 'they didn't even find a cigarette.'

A few months later, the authorities were back. This time they were looking for something entirely different. Disagreements over money had led a former Damanhurian to threaten to reveal the whereabouts of the secret temple. Unwilling to give in to blackmail, the community dug in its heels and stood by as, several times, local authority officials turned up, failed to locate the Temples of Humankind and went away again. Eventually their arch-enemy, the local magistrate, turned up with orders to drill holes and lay dynamite in the mountain. Taking a gamble, Damanhur decided to give the magistrate the full tour with all the trimmings. He tearfully emerged an hour later, a convert.

The Temples of Humankind were sequestered but placed in Damanhurian custody. In 1995, after press campaigns, internet appeals and a petition, it was declared to be a unique work of art. With a few health and safety tweaks, the installation of a lift and the obligatory gift shop, it was allowed to remain in the hands of its citizens. It even earned a place in the *Guinness Book of Records* as the 'World's Largest Underground Temple', though to be honest there's little competition in this category.

Nowadays Damanhur is more integrated into Italian society. It has a thriving economy, building eco-houses and providing some of the best organic produce for Italy's top food outlets. Its citizens remain at the forefront of environmental issues and now number more than a thousand, with support and donations from all over the world. Its reason for secretly building the world's largest underground temple is however, another story entirely. As is its claim to have built a fully-functioning time-travelling machine.

*

The name Ken Campbell usually elicits a blank response from most people. Given a bit of a nudge they might remember his cameo as the annoying Roger in *Fawlty Towers* (in the wedding anniversary episode) or several Channel 4 science documentaries in the nineties. To his dedicated followers, myself included, Ken was a hero, an intellectual genius, a fat, bald man with giant eyebrows and a voice like sandpaper, who could stand on stage delivering spellbinding comic monologues for hours. I first met him in Brighton in the mid-nineties after a show about his adventures in Damanhur and got to know him slowly over the years. A relationship with Ken wasn't easy. You didn't become friends, rather someone who Ken had frequent opportunities to perform at. But it didn't diminish my admiration for the man.

It was from one of Ken's monologues that I first heard about

The legendary Ken Campbell

Damanhur, a fantastical community that sounded straight out of the pages of a Jules Verne novel. According to Ken (and you could never be sure quite what to believe), the Damanhurians had built a university of alchemy, pioneered communication with plants and were experimenting with time travel. Like anyone whose formative years were spent glued to the telly watching Dr Who whizzing through the universe doing battle with polystyrene-clad aliens, the concept of time travel thrilled me.

The little boy in me desperately wanted to believe. I rang Ken to find out more about the place.

'You must go. Absolutely,' his voice rasped down the phone. 'Of course it's all bollocks, but magnificent bollocks.'

'You don't believe all of the things they claim?' I asked.

'I don't believe in anything. Belief is bollocks. But I'm happy to suppose in it. I suggest you do too. Entertain the idea of it being possible and it will entertain *you*. Don't get bogged down by all the technical stuff. See it as the tip of the iceberg. But listen, the Damanhurians have given me this Hollywood film script about the story of the place to edit. And that really *is* bollocks. If we're going to get Hollywood interested in Damanhur I need a good story. So here's your commission: find a man called Gorilla Eucalyptus, persuade him to take you for a ride in the time machine, have an adventure and *that* will be our new Hollywood script. I'll make sure they get Hugh Grant or someone like that to play you.' He muttered something else that sounded important.

'Sorry?'

'Oh fuck it, if you can't pay attention I'm not saying it again.' Click.

Ken's rudeness was legendary.

The other person I phoned was Ken's best mate, Jeff Merrifield. Jeff didn't quibble about belief and supposing. He had embraced all of the 'magnificent bollocks' of Damanhur and even written a book: *Damanhur: The Community They Tried to Brand a Cult*. I listened while Jeff talked about his experiences at Damanhur then dived in with a question about time travel.

'I'm very open-minded about it,' Jeff said, 'but the Damanhurians don't make a big feature of it in their lives.' There was a pause. 'Look,' he said, his voice getting more serious, 'either they didn't do it and made up a daft story, or it's real and was done for a specific purpose. But when you've achieved so many remarkable things as the Damanhurians have, why make up a story like that?'

'Have you seen the time machine?' I asked.

'Oh yes. If you're lucky you'll see it too. Listen, David, at the end of the day Damanhur is either real or the biggest con ever undertaken. Go find out for yourself.'

At Turin airport I was approached by a smiling, taciturn driver who uttered one word – 'David?' – before bundling me into his cab. We hurtled off through flat farmland of cornfields and bleached houses where angry dogs barked from behind iron gates. Roadside billboards with orange moustachioed men bore impenetrable captions: 'Hola! Funtana? 56!' I was in the northern tip of the great kinky boot of Italy, speeding towards that dark jumble of alligator teeth: the black mountains of the Alps.

'See tower?' the cabbie said after half an hour, pointing towards a light on the edge of the darkness, 'Damanhur'. After a fifteen-minute ascent we passed a sleepy mountain village, Vidracco, wound round a reservoir far below to our left and suddenly a colourful sign with a red LED display showing the temperature at a very agreeable twenty-three degrees Celsius announced that we had arrived at Damanhur's capital, Damjl.

The driver pointed me in the direction of a small wooden hut, murmured the Damanhur mantra *'con te'* (with you) and quietly left. After Ken's description of the place I was mentally prepared for a body-scan, DNA test and being forced to wear a uniform straight out of *Star Trek*.

I entered the hut apprehensively. Inside sat a young, pretty girl at a computer. Her desk was empty except for a single sheet of paper.

'Hello,' I said. The girl looked up.

'You are English? Good, you can translate lyrics for my favourite song! Who is Johnny and what are Golden Oldies?' I peered over. They were the lyrics to one of the greatest musical travesties of the twentieth century: *Walk of Life* by Dire Straits.

I had signed up for a month-long stay in a nucleo, one of the dozens of Damanhur's communal houses that dotted the mountainsides. As with Findhorn, I was about to share my life with a dozen other curious souls but this time we'd all be living in the same house together. I promised myself that this time I would reserve judgement as to whether or not they were 'my kind of people'.

The next morning, after a night in the community's B&B, I took a walk around Damjl. It had the feel of a mountain village crossed with a psychedelic ski resort and comprised of a welcome office, where I had met the Dire Straits fan, shops and accommodation for short-term visitors. Beyond these buildings a road sloped up over a small stream where strange terracotta figures perched amongst grassy knolls. The path led to an out-door temple with long lines of Grecian columns over three metres in height and in vivid orange, decorated with serpents. Between the columns were statues of ancient Greek and Egyptian gods, all handsomely endowed. On first impressions, Damanhur looked like the film set from *Clash of the Titans*.

At 10am, I was collected by Magpie, an attractive woman with a tangle of Tom Baker hair and taken to my nucleo, a few minutes' walk outside Damjl. It was a large whitewashed house with shutter-boards and set in half an acre of ground, beyond which an old dirt track led into woodlands and a small vineyard. My new family and I had signed up to a project called 'Primi Passi' (first steps), designed to acclimatise visitors to life in the community. Most of the nucleo were already there, gathered around the kitchen talking and drinking tea. I was introduced to Eroca, a slim Canadian in her fifties with shining brown eyes, two quiet young Scandinavian men and a married couple from Argentina, Christophe and Victoria, with their four-year-old son Manuel. Taking my bags up to my room, I found my roommate was already there. He was wearing wraparound shades, a black vest and jeans and was chasing a giant hornet with a beer bottle. In the corner of the room, propped up, was a familiar walking stick. It was Carel, my old roommate from Findhorn.

After a bear hug and Carel's insistence that we share a beer and a cigarette, our news was shared with the rest of the nucleo.

'It's a miracle!' Carel yelled out in the kitchen. 'When I found out this morning that David was coming I insisted we be roommates.' He threw me a huge grin. I mentally prepared myself for being woken up by him yelling out pizza toppings in his sleep but that aside, I'd forgotten how much of a big-hearted soul he was.

In the large, open-plan kitchen Magpie gathered the eleven of us together for an informal meeting.

'Well, we better get down to business,' she said.

'I have a question,' said Carel, 'I went to a bar to buy cigarettes yesterday. I said to them, "Hey, I'm staying at this crazy place called Damanhur where you can't buy cigarettes," and they said, "We're a Damanhurian bar: we don't sell cigarettes either." So I had to go into the village. What is this deal with smoking here? Why is it seen as such a bad thing?'

Magpie laughed.

'I'll leave you to find that out, Carel. But look, I got you all here to introduce yourselves. Whether you need me night or day, please call. First thing, we need someone who's willing to be coordinator for the nucleo, would anyone—'

'Yes,' said Carel.

'Thank you, Carel. And I need someone to drive, someone who—'

Carel put his hand up. 'Eh... someone else perhaps,' said Magpie.

'Ok, I will,' I said.

'What, you crazy Englishmen who drive on the left?' said Carel.

'I will,' said Christophe from Argentina.

'Thank you, Christophe,' said Magpie. 'OK Christophe, you'll be driving when needed. Carel, you'll be organising meetings. You'll need to collect money for food and other kinds of things.'

'What other kinds of things?' someone asked.

'Cigarettes,' said Carel, laughing. 'Hey, we need group song.' Putting his arms around Christophe and Eroca, Carel launched into Black Sabbath's *Paranoid*.

For the rest of the morning we were treated to a lecture on the philosophy and 'esoteric science' of Damanhur in the living room of our nucleo. It was delivered by a short man with square glasses and a passing resemblance to Dustin Hoffman. 'Damanhur was born for a magical purpose,' he began. What unfolded, complete with diagrams, was a metaphor. The Big Bang was like a shattered mirror and we were all fragments of that mirror seeking to make it whole again through our compassion. Carel made it through the first hour then slipped outside to play cowboys and Indians with the little boy Manuel instead. We could see them through the window, running around and screaming.

Like us, Damanhur's residents all lived in nucleos. These were large purpose-built communal houses, each accommodating fifteen to twenty-five people. Some worked full time in Turin, others were exclusively dedicated to the management of Damanhur. As well as sharing the cooking and cleaning in the nucleo, each member had made a commitment towards an element of personal development, agreed before the community. When this commitment was fulfilled, the resident became a fully paid-up member of Damanhur and, as such, adopted a new name.

Despite having been in an eight-year relationship with an Italian, to my shame I never learnt the basics of her native tongue. So when I first spoke over the phone to one Esperide Ananas, when arranging my visit to Damanhur, it sounded like a plausible Italian name. I would later learn that her name translated as 'Sunset Butterfly Pineapple'.

It was with great delight that, over the weeks that followed, I would discover our bespectacled lecturer was called Duck-billed Platypus Cactus and the two ladies who gave us a tour of Damjl were Salamander Olive and Hobbit Watercress. I would also meet a very tall lady called Ant Coriander and her short friend, Penguin. While residents suggested the name of the animal and plant they wanted to adopt, ultimately it was decided by committee. One alpha-male resident who fancied himself as a Panther Deadly Nightshade was given the name Dung Beetle Pansy instead. My favourites were Swordfish Banana, Beaver Pepper and Sponge Strawberry, which sounded like Jamie Oliver recipes. The Damanhurians seemed to take great delight in their singular names.

'It's all part of the game of being here,' Magpie told me, 'we approach our naming with sincerity but a sense of humour.' I could only hope that the large lady I met called Hippopotamus felt the same way too.

Each morning at our nucleo, Duck-billed Platypus Cactus would turn up and lecture for two hours. Damanhur, he taught us, was a complex and structured society, built around three integral systems. The first was the School of Meditation, which, as opposed to the Eastern approach of silent, seated contemplation, was a 'doing' meditation: applying the principle of being in the moment, such as when working on the Temples of Humankind. The second body, Social Work, was the creation and expansion of the community and the active participation of the residents in this. The third, which we would learn more about later, was called the Game of Life.

*

When told that you're going to meet a community's most accomplished musician, you don't expect them to wheel out a rubber plant. In the early eighties, Damanhur released a seven-inch single on Horus Records, featuring the music of a rubber plant called Hellie. While it didn't fare too well in the Italian charts, Hellie did go on to do a small tour of Europe and pick up a cult following. One afternoon in Damjl, Macaco Tamarind introduced our nucleo to Hellie and her 'friend', both of whom were wired up to various machines.

Macaco was in her late forties and originally from Northern Germany. A former jazz singer, she had become disillusioned with life on the road and, wanting something more extraordinary out of life, had chosen Damanhur. Macaco had been in Damanhur for more than twenty years, and spoke of the place with great passion.

'Would you like to hear Hellie singing?' she asked, with a broad smile. 'She is the best musical plant in Damanhur. She really likes to play. Here in Damanhur we have developed an electronic instrument that can translate the plant's energy into electrical impulses.'

Hellie was wired up to some archaic eighties music equipment via two crocodile clips attached to her leaves. Macaco turned on the equipment and stroked the rubber plant. Soon we began to hear long sweeps of strings mixed with the gentle tinkling of bells, like a cheesy New Age relaxation CD.

'Will the music change if she's moved or touched?' I asked.

'Yes. Come sit closer. You need to be inside her aura,' said Macaco. I began to stroke her leaves, unsure if I could sense any real change in the music and tried to resist the urge to stab her with a pen to see if the music would change into the screeching jazz of Sun Ra.

'The plants learn how to change electric conductivity to

alter the sounds. But they need a little time to practise. Now we have fig trees, roses and buttercups all making music. I like to sing with this plant,' she said, pointing at one of them in its pot. We watched in silence as Macaco leant over and did a duet with a buttercup.

At the end of the performance Macaco said, 'I have sung with her before and she was good. Today she was a little bit shy.'

Unplugging the clips and gently removing a few dead leaves from the plant, Macaco continued.

'Years ago we asked ourselves: is it possible to communicate with plants? We discovered they are very intelligent. We even put a plant on a miniature car and it was able to drive it.'

'Have you really taught plants how to drive?' Christophe

asked, a little incredulous.

'Of course. They are very cautious drivers,' Macaco added, as if that would clear up any doubts we might have had. Later we were shown photographs of the auras of an onion and a daisy, and a film of a potted plant on a miniature car crossing a busy road in Turin. The plant mounted the pavement, dodged round a few people's ankles and appeared to indulge in a spot of window-shopping and flirting with a few other plants in a local garden centre. Was this all an elaborate con? I decided to hold my peace. I would keep an open mind as Ken Campbell had suggested. 'Suppose in it and it will be more entertaining,' he'd said. Damanhur was after all, a seeker's paradise.

That evening we were invited to dinner at a guest nucleo. There I met the only Englishwoman living in Damanhur. She seemed torn between her love for the place and the things she missed about England. Once she'd started listing there was no stopping her: baked beans on toast, ketchup, salad cream, rich tea biscuits, the BBC, English pubs, villages in the Cotswolds...

'I even miss saying certain words,' she said, 'words that no one here would understand because their knowledge of English is too restricted.'

'Why not go back?' I asked.

'Because there's nothing like Damanhur in England and there never will be,' she said, scornfully, as if Britain had seriously let her down by not building an underwater temple with singing turnips and a machine that reversed the effects of balding.

'But why is no one coming over? I've been here nine years and I'm still the only Englishwoman. We've had excellent documentaries made in Denmark, Germany and Holland. Why won't the BBC make a documentary or the papers write about us? If they can't hang a good cult story on us they just don't seem interested.' She had a point. But her grumpiness was jarring. I would later discover that she had returned to the UK. The lure of tomato ketchup and *Eastenders* had just been too much.

*

Over the first week, the personality of our nucleo family began to take shape. Christophe the Argentinean took a paternal role, Eroca the Canadian grandmother played the matriarch. Carel was the teenage son and I his more responsible older brother who loved his younger sibling, envying his generosity of spirit but at the same time wishing that he could rein in some of his less appealing habits.

Christophe and his wife were at the nucleo to see if Damanhur could be their panacea. Their son, Manuel, adopted the rest of us almost immediately as his extended family. He had sword fights with me and Carel, drew pictures with Eroca in the kitchen most evenings and helped with the cooking and cleaning. I could see what a rich life a child could have growing up in a community, given freedom and responsibility, away from the media-led paranoia that if left alone to play he'd immediately be abducted by child-killers.

There was tremendous respect amongst our nucleo from the outset, despite our different nationalities and wildly differing opinions. Kevin, a tall angular Norwegian, could bring UFO conspiracy theories into the conversation even if you were talking about cornflakes. He was at Damanhur in the hope of 'learning the secrets of mind control'.

'And to avoid the aliens taking me,' he confided to me another night.

Eroca was broadening her horizons whilst travelling with her dead mother in an urn.

'She died suddenly,' Eroca explained. 'Head-on collision with a car. Mum always hated to be left out of things. She's been halfway around the world with me these last two years. She never wanted to be buried. "Just burn me up and take me wherever you go," she'd often say to me. So I did.' Most nights Eroca's mother joined us for dinner in her jar.

'Let's hope we don't mistake her for the mixed herbs,' said Carel.

Carel's role as agitator had been cemented within twenty-four hours of arriving in Damanhur. Annoyed at their attitude towards smoking, he had me take a picture of him with a fag in his mouth and holding the Damanhurian 'no smoking' sign.

'This is for the newspaper,' he said one morning. (The Damanhurians' daily paper, *Cronache*, was hand-delivered to every nucleo.) 'I am going to stage a protest.' He wrote a long letter in praise of smoking, signing himself 'The Orca Warrior' and attaching the photo I had taken.

Carel's rock and roll attitude to life had been relatively low key in Findhorn, but in Damanhur where we were living, eating and cleaning together it was more problematic. By the second week, acute toothache was making him drink heavily, he was skipping nucleo meetings (which he was supposed to be coordinating) and shirking on his cooking and cleaning obligations. Sporadically he would appear in the kitchen, regaling us with his adventures. He took photos of everything and everyone he met and would corner me in our room sometimes, put his arm around my shoulder and flick through the pictures on his digital camera, with remarks like:

'This is dentist in Valdessero, he fixed my teeth. He's got the most beautiful German Shepherd dog. This is Maria, she sold me cigarettes in Baldissero. She is nice, yes? I'm taking her for a meal tomorrow.'

One afternoon he came in hobbling, having twisted his ankle on a mountain path.

'Aw, my Achilles heel. It hurt very much,' he said. 'But I have date tonight with Maria. She's not much to look at but she has a good heart. That is more important, no?'

Ritual was a big part of the Damanhur lifestyle. The community held a special gathering each Sunday at the Temples of Humankind, regular group meditations and, once every full moon, the Summoning of the Oracle.

One evening, when a fat ivory moon hung low in the sky, Carel and I headed up to Damanhur's Open Temple at Damjl to witness it. Residents were pouring into Damjl by car from the local villages and nearby houses. At a nucleo close to the temple, men and women were changing into red and white robes. A tall robed woman began a Noah's Ark roll call:

'Aardvark, Antelope, Ant, Bison, Buffalo, Bee...'

An audience of several hundred gathered around us in the amphitheatre section of the temple, some robed, the rest sombrely attired. Ahead, the stage of the temple flickered with light. A giant crystal lay centre stage, lit from within. A crowd of robed figures hung in the background like a lynch mob waiting to strike. Shakers, gongs, bells and drums struck up. Twelve hooded figures in blue approached the stage, feeding logs to the bonfire in the centre. A strong smell of frankincense hung in the air. One of the robed women folded her arms across her chest and began to speak.

'Welcome to the ritual of the oracle. In Damanhur the oracle is not a person. By oracle we mean a growth of divine forces combining all the oracles of ancient times. The women on the stage are the priestesses who celebrate the ritual. They wear ritual robes and accessories according to the different stages of the ritual itself. The silver pointed hats represent contact with the moon and priestesses as antennae for communication with the divine. The priestess is a conduit for the responses of the divine forces.'

Then a gong was struck and everything was silent. A moment later wild shamanic drumming began. Twenty musicians sat in a line, striking different beats. Robed figures began to twist and turn to the rhythm. I quickly fell under the spell of the ritual and the rhythms of the music, transported back to Ancient Greece. The branches the moon goddesses had thrown in the fire began to take shape before me. Were strange creatures twisting themselves out of the fire? I couldn't draw my eyes away. Then, out of the blue, I heard the theme tune to *Hawaii Five-O*. And so did a hundred other people, as they turned to where Carel and I were sat, rolling their eyes.

'Oh shit,' said Carel and, stick in hand, scuttled off to answer his mobile phone.

*

The Damanhurians liked to refer to themselves as 'a nation of builders'. It was apt. As well as the village of Damjl and the Temples of Humankind, in 2003 Damanhur acquired an abandoned Olivetti factory nearby and, in less than a year, transformed it into their own unique visitors' complex-cum-shopping-mall called 'Crea'. Besides its artists' studios were a conference hall, secondary school, hairdresser, dentist, laboratory, cocktail bar and GM-free supermarket, which only ever seemed to be piping out that grisly European eighties hit *Live is Life*. The walls of Crea were decorated with hundreds of paintings by Damanhur's founder, Falco. They looked like the daubings of a Glastonbury raver but were, according to the Damanhurians, magical.

The basement of Crea housed a workshop, run by two well-dressed middle-aged women. The shop was full of delicate wire-cutters, soldering irons and other tools as the ladies diligently hand-crafted strange creations known as *selficas*, which looked like artefacts from another world. According to Sunset Butterfly Pineapple, the 'world expert in selfic devices', they were batteries powered by a unique energy source.

'Selficas are based on an ancient energy system from Atlantis. Unlike batteries they are intelligent because they can interact with you.'

They were made of copper wiring, glass, alchemical liquid and gold leaf. Around the shop were selficas for neck pain, 'women's problems' and one attached to a pen for automatic writing. Joy selficas could 'diffuse joy for a radius of up to twelve metres'. The most expensive, at €10,000, was for contacting the planet Venus. (Selficas could also be mistaken for futuristic-looking bombs, as I was later to discover when trying to take one back through customs at Gatwick.)

Selfic devices were an important part of Damanhur life. Every member of the community wore a selfic bracelet, some had selficas on the dashboards of their cars. More surprising still, the same copper wiring ran along the ceilings of nucleos and other buildings like bare electrical cable. Thirty tons of this cabling was said to converge at a great circuit board deep inside the temple, powering the Temples of Humankind with selfic energy.

An intrinsic part of selfic design was the spiral. It was the symbol most closely associated with Damanhur. The community had even built great spirals in the mountainsides out of coloured stones. Visitors were invited to walk these spirals 'for healing purposes', though once when I went to wander round

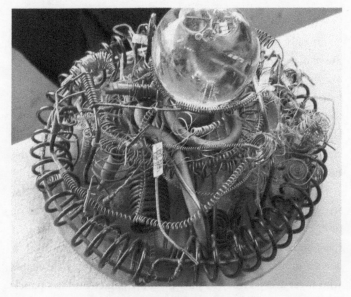

Selfica

one after a lunch at a hilltop nucleo, Sunset Butterfly Pineapple shouted at me:

'David, David, have you opened it with the key?'

'Er, no. What key?' I said. As far as I could see it was just a spiral of stones in a field.

'Oh no! Come out of there at once!'

Feeling like a naughty schoolboy I left the spiral.

'What's wrong?'

'What's wrong? Without the key you deactivate the spiral. With the spiral deactivated you shut down the Temples of Humankind.'

'And what does that mean?'

'It only means, David, that you risk sending the whole of the planet back on a path of self-destruction.'

I suspect that by now that you're probably full of questions as to what the hell was going on at Damanhur. Singing plants? Underground temples? Destruction of the Earth? It's time to clear things up a little. But to do that, we need to travel into the future by several hundred years. Hold onto your hat!

It's 2600 AD (or thereabouts) and the Earth has been destroyed by a bunch of alien mind-hackers who, in an act of pure malice, have taken away humankind's free will and sent the planet on a path of destruction. Observing this from a corner of the galaxy is a group of interplanetary delegates who meet every Friday as part of some galactic affairs panel. They lament the destruction of Earth but, like David Attenborough filming his nature documentaries, have long ago agreed to observe and report but not to get involved in the affairs of other species. One of them has a particular fondness for the people of Earth however and decides we deserve a sporting chance. He travels back in time to 1950 and has himself 'preincarnated' into the body of a human baby in Turin called Oberto Airaudi. At a young age Airaudi realises his mission in life is to save mankind from destruction. Despite a brief spell as an insurance salesman, Airaudi soon gets to the job in hand, amassing a small group of followers to build a giant battery to jolt the Earth onto a new timeline. But the only place this can be done is on the Earth's 'synchronic knot' (a meeting point of the Earth's four 'rivers of energy'). And first it has to be located. So the team set off round the world looking for it. If it had been in Central Park or under the Bull Ring in Birmingham they'd have been scuppered but, as luck would have it, they finally find the synchronic knot located less than an hour's drive from Turin. Better still, the land is for sale. The giant battery is to become the Temples of Humankind, built into a rare but highly conductive rock strata (mylonite) over a thirty-year period and powered by selfic energy.

After a series of complex rituals and building of stone spirals, the Earth's new timeline is created and the Earth is saved. Its people now have free will to decide their own fate, thanks to the Damanhurians. But like a rail track or busy road, a timeline is prone to needing repairs and upkeep. But where do you go to get the nuts and bolts to maintain a new timeline? The nearest place that sells them is a little shop in Atlantis. And to get there you'd need to travel back in time. This is why the Damanhurians don't like to make a big fuss about building a time machine: they only really use it for shopping.

*

The coach bounced and careered its way up a treacherous mountain path. I was with Christophe, Victoria and Eroca, on our way to see the Temples of Humankind for the first time. My belly tingled with excitement. Our driver, Swordfish Banana, drove with the recklessness of a man familiar with every sharp turn and pothole. We wound through dusty cliff faces and patchy woodlands until we arrived at a nucleo, one we hadn't visited before. There was no evidence of what lay below our feet. Standing outside, waiting for us was our guide, Sunset Butterfly Pineapple. She led us into a small utility room in the nucleo, where we donned plastic coverings for our feet. From here we were led down a corridor. The corridor went on. And on. It was like the wardrobe in Narnia. Hieroglyphics began to appear on the walls. At the end of the corridor stood a lift. After descending into the lift we emerged into the bowels of the mountain.

We were standing in two large split-level circular rooms, filled with dazzling colour and light. The walls were decorated with collages of people and animals. In the centre of the room a sculpted column of white marble ran from floor to the ceiling, decorated with signs of the zodiac and tiny lights. Towering images of naked bodies filled the walls. On the floor around the room were hundreds of pottery figurines like an Antony Gormley exhibition. Sunset Butterfly turned out the lights and we were left standing in the dark below the stars.

'This is a sky map, with optical fibres representing the stars as they would have been seen twenty thousand years ago,' she said. 'The temple is a 3D book that can be read. Everything you need to know about Damanhur is written on these walls.' We travelled deeper, down dimly-lit stone corridors to the Hall of Spheres where nine coloured crystal balls were set into enclaves, representing nine divinities. Butterfly pressed her hand knowingly into a stone slab in the wall and, as the sound of hydraulics kicked in, a heavy stone door creaked open its secrets. It was pure Indiana Jones.

We were now in the labyrinth, a criss-cross of corridors and mirrored walls that stretched off into the distance. On the walls were back-lit, stained-glass windows depicting the faces of hundreds of different gods. Down one corridor I noticed Hobbit Watercress halfway up a ladder, painting a wall. 'Work in progress,' said Butterfly.

We journeyed on. Egyptian paintings, used as code to decipher secret doorways, appeared in many of the passageways. Walls slid back, staircases appeared, each chamber more stunning than the last, reminding me of the catacombs of Paris and the Hagia Sophia in Istanbul. We reached another that looked like a cross between Frankenstein's lab and Dr McCoy's medical room on the USS *Enterprise*. Over a hundred selfic devices hung over a hospital bed.

'For treating incurable diseases,' Butterfly explained. On the wall was a giant map of the Earth's synchronic lines, converging at Damanhur.

Our final destination was a small, round chamber. From the ceiling hung a circle of long glass tubes full of bubbling liquids. A giant magnetic strip coiled around the walls. There was space inside the circle of tubes for a person to stand. On the wall, a painting of a golden serpent coiled upwards, snaking its way around bizarre symbols, like the doodlings of a mad Egyptian scientist.

'This is a selfic cabin,' Butterfly said, 'the potential of this structure is very, very high. It is possible to use this for experiments for widening perception... lucid dreams... therapy.'

Having pestered her since the beginning of the tour, Sunset

Butterfly pre-empted my question.

'Is this –?'

'Yes David, this is the time machine.'

Whilst missing the all-important on/off lever and analogue time display, Damanhur's time machine would still have delighted the most ardent science-fiction fan.

'Can I just step–'

'No,' laughed Sunset Butterfly, pulling me away.

At the end of the tour we surfaced to find a thunderstorm raging over the Alps. It only served to re-enforce the feeling that I was in some epic adventure movie, an alternative reality beyond my comprehension. Quite unexpectedly, I burst into tears.

'Don't worry, it's a common reaction,' said Butterfly.

Damanhur's time machine

Damanhur's founder, Falco, was a brown-eyed man with an inscrutable expression and thinning, dyed black hair. It was hard to believe that Damanhur had come about because of this man's singular vision. When facing an audience, he looked ill at ease, fidgeting and twitching as if he couldn't wait for the moment when he could stand up and bolt for the door. Permanently attired in jeans and a shabby zip-up cardigan, he looked more like the kind of man who'd lecture in Systems Analysis at Doncaster University than the leader of a new civilisation.

The Damanhurians went to great lengths to assert that Falco was not a guru. He would himself chastise the community if they treated him like a father figure and would occasionally disappear for weeks on end to encourage their sense of independence.

Most Friday evenings at Damjl during the month that I was there, Falco held a press conference with an English translator. This was the one opportunity I had to give him a good grilling with the endless array of questions that had been building up since arriving. Despite Ken Campbell's insistence that I 'don't get bogged down by all the technical stuff' I had quickly come to the same conclusion as him: Damanhur was 'magnificent bollocks'. But while it had all the trappings of a cult – revered leader, crazy beliefs, terrible artwork – its residents were so disarmingly down-to-earth, intelligent and compassionate, there was something about the place that just didn't add up. The stories about Damanhur were truly bonkers; my initial impression was that the same couldn't be said for its residents and founders.

A few of our nucleo, Carel included, crammed into a small room where Falco was miked up and sat in front of a camera. I was permitted to ask the first question. 'This will clear things up once and for all,' I thought to myself.

'Falco, I hear lots of different stories about you. That you're an alien who travelled back in time, that you understand how to harness the energies of Atlantis and have built a time machine. My question is, which of these, if any, are true?' There was a brief murmur in the room. Falco smiled, nodded and answered:

'I'm just someone trying to do my best. We all come from different places.'

'Bastard! He answered like a politician!' I whispered to Eroca next to me.

'Perhaps he's just playing with you,' she replied.

'Why keep time travel a secret?' asked an elderly German journalist.

'It would be disastrous in the wrong hands!' laughed Falco, making it clear that was all he was prepared to say on the subject. Next it was Carel's turn to speak.

'How come you are so concerned about smoking? You permit cars on the premises, which create more pollution, yet smokers can't even smoke outside. Inside the buildings I understand, but outside?'

Falco curled his lips into a slight smile and replied that cigarette smoke was bad for the environment and that Damanhur was doing all it could to change to eco-friendly fuel for cars.

'If you smoke, stop smoking. It's a discipline required here,' he concluded. But Carel hadn't finished with him.

'And what if I wage war on Damanhur and set up my own Utopia *inside* Damjl where smoking is permitted?'

'We will fight you and we will win,' replied Falco firmly.

An American visitor spoke next.

'My name is Mary, I'm travelling the world for peace. I am a journalist. A free spirit. Someone told me that all my astrology was here. I would like to write a road map and peace songs that would make a movie. I am a child of Hollywood. I am from California. And my question is: "Who built Stonehenge?"'

*

It hadn't taken me long to realise that there was a conspiracy of silence at Damanhur surrounding time travel. As with my experience with Falco, questions were either deflected, or responses ambiguous. The only thing I'd learned so far was that part of the training to be a 'temponaut' was 'practising how to hold in your shit'.

'You can't go back in time shitting everywhere,' one of the Damanhurians said to me, 'think of the risk of spreading modern diseases'.

When news of their fantastical claim was first made public, Damanhur *had* initially been quite open. One resident, Gorilla Eucalyptus, described in detail his experiences travelling back to the year 4719 BC in a special 'time-travel edition' of *Kindred Spirit* magazine. It even included a short article from the Damanhurians called '*How Time Travel Works*, which began: 'Time is conceptualised as a circular sea of eternal present where all the events are at the same time, but also as a flux moving in the direction of complexity.'

It continued in a similarly oblique vein.

When discussing Damanhur's time machine with other people, Ken Campbell took delight in asking:

'What percentage chance would you give that it actually works?'

When he'd asked me, I'd responded:

'I don't know... one per cent?' to which Ken had snorted:

'Fuck me, as much as that? You can use decimal places.'

And while I couldn't 'suppose' that time travel had been quietly figured out by a small band of Italians, a part of me, the little boy who was once obsessed with Dr Who, really wished it had. Then I could have acted out a fantasy in which, with the help of Gorilla Eucalyptus, I would steal the time machine and travel back in time a sufficient number of years to save my relationship *and* give Ken the Hollywood script he was looking for. If only.

*

Shortly after the press conference with Falco, Carel had disappeared, off on yet another rendezvous at a local bar. Later that night, driving back from the supermarket with Christophe, I spotted him blind drunk, miles from the house, while cars careered around him on the dark, steep mountain paths. Christophe pulled over in the van.

'Want a lift home, my friend?' he asked.

'Come to party!' yelled Carel.

'What party?' I asked.

'It's in Turin, that's all I know,' Carel said, pointing into the blackness and silence of the Alps. Christophe and I looked at each other. Turin was sixty miles away. We dragged Carel into the van and drove him back to the nucleo. After a short wrestling match in our room with Kevin the Norwegian, he finally passed out. The next morning I awoke early to find a note on the kitchen table. It read:

> **Dear friends,**
> **I took my grandfather's walking stick and I'm on my way for a walkabout in the beautiful nature and mountains around. I'm also on the warpath against certain aspects of the Damanhur mentality. It's not a war of blood and poison, it's a mind war, and I believe we will all get better from it. One way or another. The battle has begun. They drew first blood.**
> *Carel, the Orca Warrior*

As well as skipping our nucleo meetings and morning lectures, Carel had also been refusing to take part in any activities or rituals at Damanhur that demanded payment. Here I admired his principles. Damanhur had a tendency to put a price on everything, despite our having already paid to be there. We had paid ten Euros to hear Falco speak one Thursday evening and a further ten to become a 'spiritual person of Damanhur' (a ten-minute ceremony that involved being given a pink thread). When it was understood that in visiting another nucleo for dinner we were also obliged to pay, Carel had said:

'I feel deeply uncomfortable when a transaction like this goes on when someone is feeding me in their own house. That's not how we do it in Belgium. I don't mind buying a bottle of wine or gift of equivalent price but you don't visit someone's house for a meal and give them money.' I had to agree.

The following evening, when the majority of our nucleo were out having dinner in the nearby village, I had opted to stay behind with Eroca to make a soup. As we were preparing the vegetables Carel appeared in the kitchen doorway, wearing just his little woolly hat, underpants and vest. He had been sleeping in his room all afternoon, recovering from another operation on his gums. He was clearly in a lot of pain still. We gave him some soup and – as was his habit – he started flicking through his photographs from the day.

'Here's me with the dentist... this is the car I got a lift home in... here's the bottle of Bud I got for free last night from the barman...'

He rested his grandfather's weathered stick on the table and fidgeted with a carrot, wincing occasionally and holding the side of his face. Then, looking intently at us, he put his spoon down and said:

'Did I ever tell you how my grandfather died?'

Carel's dad had been only eleven months old when his own father was murdered. Before the Second World War his grandfather had been a trader and when the war started he moved into smuggling: food, goods, people, whatever was on offer.

While playing his part by smuggling Jews out of the country he was also lining his pocket.

'He was doing it for money you understand, not for love,' Carel said, 'he was the kind of man who saw the price in everything. By all accounts he was also a bear of a man, with brute strength and a lot of pent-up anger. Sure he hated the Germans but he could also be violent towards my grandmother and his own children. One day my uncle and his elder brother challenged him. "If you ever hurt her again we will kill you," they said. He stopped after that.

'One day some Flemish soldiers of the SS drove into town. They were thirsty; they had been on the road all day. They were looking for something to drink and approached my grandfather's sister, who ran a shop.

'"Can we have some water from you?" they asked. She took one of the soldiers down into the cellar to collect the water and he noticed that she had some milk there too.

'"We would like milk. Can I buy milk instead?" he asked.

'As the soldier was saying this, my grandfather appeared at the top of the stairs. He was in a foul mood and, mistaking the soldiers as Germans, spoke to his sister in Flemish, chastising her for selling milk to soldiers.

'"What do you want to do that for?" he said, "selling milk to scum like this? Better put poison in it first and do the world a favour."

'At this, the soldier ran out shouting, "Resistance! Resistance!"

'No one really knows what happened next but one of the

soldiers had been banging on a door in the village with his rifle when a gun went off. The soldier fell to the floor with a wound. Did his rifle backfire on him or had the resistance picked him off? We still don't know to this day but the soldiers reacted by rounding up all the men between eighteen and twenty-five in the village, marching them to a nearby trench in the woods and gunning them all down. Every one of them was killed. Most other people in the village had fled by this time but my uncle, hidden in the trees, saw it all. My grandfather was one of those men they murdered. Last year my father received pictures of the dead men in the trench. Someone in the village had photographed it. I have those pictures here on my camera now. You know, when my father saw those pictures for the first time he stood before me with tears in his eyes and said, "I love you son."

'It was the first time he had ever said that to me. Now when we talk we have real conversations, not just chitchat about football and fishing. But why does it take something of that magnitude just to tell someone that you love them?'

Close to the end of my residency, our nucleo was asked to give a short presentation on stage after one of Falco's Q&As. 'Succinct but entertaining' was the brief. We decided to say our thank yous then do a silly Egyptian dance. This was at the request of Christophe, a natural comedian.

Despite being guests that night in the hall, our nucleo were still asked to pay five Euros each. Unsurprisingly, Carel was absent.

Falco arrived in his trademark cardigan. He waved off the audience's attempt to stand and seemed far more convivial than the previous times I'd seen him on stage in Crea. What followed was an hour-long discussion amongst the Daman-hurians that seemed to be a game of one-upmanship as to who could spout the most esoteric New Age psychobabble. As far as I could gather, a man called Dingo was talking about building an astral library that would take off full of informa-tion, cross space, touch a series of orbits and return again.

At 8.30, Anaconda introduced our nucleo. We left our seats and walked onto the stage singing a song that Eroca had taught us. The audience gave a polite clap. Then we arranged ourselves into a line, Manuel included, ready to say our thanks.

It was then that we noticed Carel. Like the star of his own eighties pop video, he flung open the doors at the back of the hall, dramatically stubbed out a fag on the floor and came running through the auditorium in woolly hat, vest, shades and waving his walking stick. Before we knew it Carel had bounded onto the stage, grabbed the microphone and, twirling his stick above his head, began to shout:

'I want to tell you a story. From a long time ago. It's a story about Atlantis.'

The audience looked blankly at the drunken Belgian. Carel began to croon his favourite Iron Maiden song. 'I'm not a num-ber, I'm a free man,' he warbled, pacing the stage. The sound man, taking this as his cue, started the music for our dance. *Walk Like an Egyptian* began to play. As Carel continued wailing his metal anthem, our ensemble, not knowing what else to do, broke into its Egyptian dance.

'I'm not a number, I'm a free man!' Carel continued scream-ing into the microphone, and began lobbing cigarettes into the audience. For the next three gruelling minutes, the rest of us wiggled our arses and conga-ed our way around the stage.

Afterwards, as we were leaving, a woman who'd been sitting in the front row came over to me and said, 'I'm very sorry but I'm not sure what it is you were trying to convey tonight. Perhaps it was lost in translation?'

'Perhaps so,' I said. 'I have similar problems with these evenings too.'

We headed back to our nucleo just after midnight. Fuelled by beers and the need to walk off pasta, we had left the van at Crea and opted instead for the precarious half-hour walk to our home along the left-hand side of the dark mountainous road where a small stone wall was the only divide between us and the blackness of the reservoir hundreds of metres below. When a car approached we would huddle against the wall until it passed – we knew from experience that Italian drivers could be reckless, even on these dangerous roads. After gate-crashing our gig, Carel had gone off to his favourite bar where smoking was permitted, so our conversation was dominated with his impromptu performance, which was told and retold amongst great peals of laughter. There was a great deal of love for Carel amongst our nucleo.

A distant hoot turned the conversation to owls and I told the story of my friend Chris, who had been walking home late one night in a sleepy London suburb when he felt a sharp pain on the top of his head. Putting his hand up he felt blood and whirled around to confront his aggressor, but the street appeared empty. Bewildered and a little shaken, he happened to pass the local police station and so wandered in and described what had happened. The policeman behind the counter listened patiently, nodding his head and gave a one-word explanation: 'owls'. It seemed the local tawny was getting a bit cheesed off with people wandering into its turf and had taken to dive-bombing their heads and sticking his claws in.

'Ya, I had a very strange encounter with owls once,' said Nils the quiet Dane. Suddenly a car came hurtling round the corner and we all stepped against the wall to take refuge. All except Nils. Where the wall should have been there was simply a hole. His body began to slip into the darkness, arms flailing. Eroca, who'd been standing next to him, grabbed his hand and she began to get pulled over too. Several hands reached for her at once and together we pulled them both up. A second later and Nils and Eroca would have been tumbling down into the murky blackness, never to be seen again. Nils and Eroca stood there shaking and hugging each other.

'You saved my life,' he said, in his understated Norwegian way, but the shock and gratitude was evident.

'It was all of us,' said Eroca, 'I would have tumbled over there with you if it hadn't been for David, Christophe and Victoria.'

The rest of us remained silent in the darkness until Christophe said:

'I think this calls for a group hug'. We squeezed each other tight and our mass of bodies shook from the trembling we all still felt at what might have been. For the rest of the journey home we were quiet. We had played support act to a drunken Belgian and saved the lives of two of our own. We never did get to hear Nils's strange owl story.

During the last evening together, our nucleo set up party games in the lounge area of our home. Everyone took part, including Carel. Despite an average age range of nearly sixty years, we played wink murder and musical statues, told bad jokes, danced like imbeciles and ended up with our heads on each other's bellies in a wide circle laughing like lunatics. Christophe wrapped up the night with a short speech.

'I went to buy some bread the other morning and I noticed the person from the store out the back doing a quick ritual, acknowledging the four corners of the world with a prayer. I wish everywhere I go in the world I see the guy from the grocery store doing that.'

It was clear how much we were all going to miss each other. As with Findhorn, the time shared with people had, again, been the most rewarding part of the trip for me. There had been little in the way of personality clashes, or the inevitable bickering when a group of people are forced to live together and make collective decisions. Instead there had been respect, generosity, openness and demonstrations of incredible patience towards Carel. He disappeared at all times of day and night, turned up inebriated, regularly woke us up in the small hours and did what he pleased with little consideration for how it might impact on the rest of us. On several occasions, he failed to materialise after having agreed to cook for the nucleo, leaving us hungry and despondent. And don't get me started on his snoring. But equally he was principled, took people on face value, stood up for what he believed in (even if it was unpopular), had a big heart and a filthy sense of humour.

Living with him for the second time, I had begun to see some of my own selfish behaviour in the past reflected back at me. Through Carel's reluctance to compromise for the sake of others, I realised how much I had put myself first in my relationship with my ex and with others who cared about me. I could feel myself starting to change.

Over the last month, our nucleo's kitchen had been alive with confessional, bizarre and 'putting the world to rights' conversations. Both Nils and I shed tears on separate nights, sharing our heartache and regrets from recent break-ups, eliciting group hugs and sympathy. Thanks to Eroca's interest in the subject we debated tantric sex as a 'new sexual revolution', argued vehemently about the 9/11 conspiracies (I think they're all tosh), the legalisation of recreational drugs (I'm in favour) and listened patiently to Kevin's theory of how humankind descended from space monkeys. But the most repeated topic of conversation was the issue of Damanhur's fantastical claims, a topic which I was hellbent on steering back to again and again. I tested the patience of my nucleo by asking the same questions: Did the plants actually sing? Was the time machine real? Did they really believe Falco was an alien? It seemed to bother *me* far more than everyone else. Christophe said:

'David, do you *really* care if Falco is from the future or if he went to Atlantis or not? He's not playing the guru, he lives in a community like everyone else and seems to be a humble and intelligent man. Look around you, David. See what is real here. And ask yourself a more important question; do you like what you see in Damanhur?'

I did like what I saw. But I'd been living in a house for four weeks decorated with images of Atlantis that were supposedly painted by a friend of one of their time-travellers, Gorilla Eucalyptus, who'd hitched a ride into the distant past with his paintbrush and easel. Wouldn't any sane person feel the need to question this stuff?

The lightbulb moment came for me one afternoon in Damanhur's bookshop when Magpie and Goat were showing off *Le Storie di Damanhur*, an illustrated hardback book that the community had recently published. It was laid out cartoon-style, like an Asterix book.

'The story, or myth, of Damanhur,' said Magpie, translating the title for me. The book began with the description of how a bright star was taken as a good omen to Falco and his disciples on the mountain one night, leading to a decision to start building the Temples of Humankind.

'Why not call it the history of Damanhur?' I asked.

'Ah. Good question!' she said, laughing. 'Because these stories are whatever you want them to be. They're our myth. It doesn't matter whether you take them literally. It's really not important. At Damanhur we ask only if our myth connects with you.'

Goat nodded in agreement, adding:

'We're here to understand the purpose of community because that is how we can best be mirrors for each other. This myth gives us a sense of direction. It's about humanity. Myth gives you inner connection with what a community is built for. If you want to have a satisfying life, you need a sense of purpose. You have to choose to play that game and not be played. In the end what you will have lived is a really good life. Maybe that will count more than the uncertainty. But you have to play everything, spare nothing or you'll never know. Living this kind of life changes people. It leads to a life you can die with.'

*

I've since come to believe that Damanhur has created something extraordinary and unique in the modern world.

In his TV series from the eighties, *The Power of Myth*, writer Joseph Campbell discussed how our old religions and myths have failed us, which is why they are being discarded. But while science is the best language we have for *explaining* the universe, he argued, what the world desperately needs now are more modern myths, new myths to teach us *how* to live.

Anyone going to Damanhur seeking concrete evidence of time travel will be disappointed: it's not how the place works. Much as I'd have loved to, I wouldn't be fulfilling Ken's commission to 'steal the time machine and have an adventure' to help with his Hollywood script. And Gorilla Eucalyptus had long since left the community. Damanhur wasn't simply 'magnificent bollocks'. And it was more than just a medicine show or theme park. It was a modern-day story of Biblical proportions, packed with parables of time travel, malevolent aliens and the destruction of the Earth. Damanhur was a living myth. It had built a glorious film set of epic proportions, in which its residents chose their roles and, together, wrote the script. As with any great myth or religion, some members had taken it (too) literally, others saw it is a metaphor for how they should live their lives. Like ancient civilisations of the past, its residents immersed themselves in their myth and used it to set themselves important life-changing challenges. For those whom the myth of Damanhur resonated, perhaps it really could be some kind of Utopia.

The brilliance of Damanhur didn't stop there. One of the greatest contributions to its continued growth and success was through the Game of Life. Aware of the very real problem of inertia in intentional communities, Damanhur was constantly looking for ways to offer new and challenging experiences for its citizens. Each nucleo, acting as a kind of benevolent Big Brother, kept a watchful eye on the levels of happiness and personal growth of its neighbours. Should it be noted that a nucleo was getting a bit complacent, staying in every night drinking sherry and watching re-runs of *Six Feet Under*, it could get a call from the Game of Life team.

As Duck-billed Platypus explained it, 'You can be called upon any time of day or night to leave your home and go away for an unforeseen amount of time. You won't know where you are going and are not allowed to inform friends. It requires absolute trust of course but challenges and transformations can be incredible. Plus it's a great deal of fun.'

The very first Game of Life activity attracted world press back in the eighties when fourteen Damanhurians were set the challenge to survive on a mountain for six months with only the very basic of tools. At the end of their experiment the ones who stuck it out had learned to live entirely off their immediate environment, including how to fashion their own clothes and shoes. Several chose to remain in the wild for another year. Soon after, another nucleo was set the challenge to build a village in the trees. Within a year they had realised the possibility of an arboreal existence, with log cabins nestled high in what Damanhurians called the 'Sacred Wood', connected by a network of rope bridges.

One afternoon, Beaver Pepper informed me that Damanhur was 'now engaged in intelligent conversation with the trees'.

'Anything to report?' I'd asked, flippantly.

'Well, yes,' Beaver said. 'We've discovered that trees hate being hugged. It makes them feel cold, uncomfortable and it drains them of their natural energy. They've kindly asked us all to stop.' I promised to spread the word.

As a seeker, Damanhur surpassed all of my expectations. It was an epic play that you could turn up to and choose yourself a role. The only thing missing was a good hot tub or two, perched on the mountainside. Could it be my Utopia? I certainly took great delight in the thought of phoning up my family to let them know I'd joined a community of time-travellers in

the Alps and from now on wished to be known as 'Chaffinch Lemongrass'. But then, being hopeless at learning languages, would I have the same problem as the grumpy English-woman? I could get by without salad cream and ketchup, but I'd also miss the nuances of conversation in my mother tongue. One thing I *was* sure of: Damanhur was a place to which I would return.

*

It would be disingenuous to claim that my search for a better life was in any way original. At least I was in good company. For millennia, the concept of Utopia has been debated by philosophers, yearned for by the masses and ridiculed by satirists. It can be traced back as far as Plato who in 360 BC envisaged a model society and called it *Republic* in his book of the same name. (On reflection, he later admitted, it was a bit of a crap title and wished he'd gone for *Platopolis*.) The book takes the form of a Socratic dialogue: reported conversations from lively and drunken debates known as symposiums between various members of the Greek intelligentsia.

In *Republic* it is Socrates, Plato's mentor, who always comes up trumps in the debates. Through Socrates' voice, Plato tackles the tricky subject of social justice and how to find a balance between the needs of the individual and the needs of others. Socrates defines the citizens of the Republic as fitting into one of three categories: producers, warriors or guardians. Producers, he argues, are no good at running a society, as they're led by their base desires and will be too busy indulging in 'wine, women and song' to make informed decisions. (Unsurprisingly, artists and actors are included in this category too.) Warriors are also considered unsuitable for the task. Controlled by their emotions, Socrates argues, they're far too unpredictable. Instead, he concludes, society is best left in the hands of guardians, an oligarchy of elected philosopher rulers with a shared knowledge and wisdom of the 'common good'. Had this ever come to fruition during his lifetime, Socrates would undoubtedly have done lots of throat clearing and pointing at himself during the elections. For his time, he was also a radical feminist, insisting these rulers should be both men and women.

So far, so good, but at the end to everyone's surprise Socrates announces that poets would be banished from the Republic because they appeal to the 'basest part of the soul'. One can only conclude that either Plato's publisher advised him to put a 'good twist' at the end or that someone had once written a rude poem about him.

While Plato's *Republic* still has plenty to offer on the subject of ethics, to a modern Westerner this 'model society' may well come across as a crude caste system, ruled by an academic elite and crossed with the worst aspects of communism. Hardly appealing, unless you happen to be a philosophy tutor with a messianic complex.

The word *'utopia'* does not appear in Plato's *Republic*. In fact it didn't come into existence until almost two thousand years later when it was conceived as a pun by the English statesman and writer Sir Thomas More, for his book of the same name. Exactly how much of More's *Utopia* was intended as satire has long been debated by academics. The Latin word *utopia* has two pronunciations and meanings:

ee-yoo-topia (a sweet place)
oo-topia (no place)

The story tells of a fictional meeting between Thomas More and his real-life friend Peter Giles in Antwerp. Giles introduces More to a sunburnt, bearded stranger, Raphael Hythloday, a philosopher and traveller who, after a hearty lunch, describes in detail his favourite place, Utopia, an isthmus in Asia that has become an island. Utopia, Hythloday declares, is peaceful, tolerant of different religious practises and treats communal property as superior to individual ownership. Its citizens, having little use for frivolous materials like gold, use it to make bedpans. (The joke here is that they eschew gold by shitting on it. To be honest the jokes don't get any better than this.)

By the Middle Ages in Europe, the peasants had dreamed up their own 'loser's' paradise': the Land of Cockaigne, a medieval meme that first appears in English in the poem *The Land of Cockaygne* collected in the '*Kildare Poems*' in the fourteenth century. The Land of Cockaigne was a bucolic idyll, whose residents sat around gorging themselves and drinking to excess. Rivers of beer, milk and wine flowed through its valleys. Its abbeys were made of meat pies. Those who couldn't be bothered to cook would just open their mouths and in would fly a freshly cooked lark, seasoned with a nice bit of cinnamon. In the Land of Cockaigne the population was eternally young and sex was readily available to all. Those deluded enough to go in search of Cockaigne would have headed to the west of Spain where it was believed to exist. Even if they had found it, the messy entrance requirements would have given them second thoughts:

> Heavy penance he must face;
> The man who hopes to share its bliss
> For seven years, be sure of this,
> Must wade through pigshit to his chin,
> The pleasures of Cockaigne to win.

In the latter part of the second millennium, the horrors of the Industrial Revolution brought a new wave of Utopianists. William Morris, Edward Bellamy and Samuel Butler wrote of socialist Utopias that sought to undo the brutality of the 'dark satanic mills'. These new worlds were places where citizens did jobs that nourished their creativity and souls, allowing them time for leisure pursuits and artistic endeavours.

By the early twentieth century, ecology, machinery and feminism began to become part of the utopian framework too. Charlotte Perkins Gilman described a peaceful world run entirely by women in *Herland*, while H.G. Wells wrote of a mechanised leisure society in his rather unimaginatively titled novel *A Modern Utopia*. In the early sixties, as an antidote to *Brave New World*, Aldous Huxley wrote *Island*, heavily influenced by his involvement with the burgeoning New Age scene and interest in Eastern mysticism. The inhabitants of Huxley's island, Pala, practised group living, free love, took psychedelic plants to improve their intellect and undoubtedly wore kaftans. They even trained parrots to fly around the island and call out 'uplifting messages' every five minutes such as 'Concentrate on the here and now'. Huxley hadn't really thought this last bit through. (Nowadays it would be like a really annoying ring-tone going off every few minutes.) Were Pala a real place, it would only be a matter of time before its residents were gorging themselves on parrot stew.

After the wars and genocide instigated by Hitler, Stalin, Pol Pot, Mao Tse-tung and other tyrants of the twentieth century, utopian thinking fell out of fashion. It even became a dirty word in academic circles. Communism and fascism, once seen by many as utopian ideals, had seriously failed us.

In our post-modern age, utopian novels continue to be on the decline. But then there is an inherent problem with utopian fiction: it's rather dull. Imagining a place where everyone is happy, there's no conflict and nothing to struggle for is hardly an exciting premise for a story. No conflict means no drama. Dystopian tales however, continue to be hugely popular. But do we really need more doom and gloom in our Prozac-popping twenty-first century? Haven't we all at different times in our lives imagined a better world? For me, no one has argued the case for utopianism so persuasively and succinctly as Oscar Wilde.

'A map of the world that does not include Utopia is
not worth even glancing at, for it leaves out the one
country at which Humanity is always landing. And
when Humanity lands there, it looks out and, seeing
a better country, sets sail. Progress is the realisation
of Utopias.' *Oscar Wilde*

CHAPTER 6

The Land of Milk and Honey

How some English friends of mine can hate Americans is a mystery. OK, their foreign policy and fondness for line-dancing may be questionable, but at least they *like* the English.

I once spent a very uncomfortable evening in a comedy club in Dublin when the compère asked if anyone was from out of town and my ex, in her naivety, called out:

'Yes, England!' We were duly booed.

And a friend of mine still pretends he's Welsh to his Scottish in-laws to avoid any unpleasantness over Christmas dinner.

Americans don't just *like* us, they romanticise us: envying our history, fawning over our accents and making us feel attractive and interesting simply for having been born on one particular cold, damp island. Having finished my travels around Europe

I was now on my way to the west coast of America, about to discover the delights of being an Englishman alone in a land of zealous anglophiles.

I was lost in the backstreets of the Tenderloin in a hire car. It's hardly San Francisco's most salubrious district. Jetlagged, I just wanted to find my hotel and have an afternoon nap. Despite adopting my dad's bloody-minded attitude of driving round lost for hours rather than asking a stranger for help, I eventually cracked. I wound the window down and asked a young woman laden with shopping for directions to Guerrero Street. She smiled.

'English! Where are you from?'

'Brighton.'

'I've been there! You have that Indian palace right? And all those pretty villages.' I nodded. 'Where were you born?'

'You wouldn't know it, it's a town called Scunthorpe.' A wistful look came over her.

'I bet it's beautiful.'

'Erm, yes.' If you like concrete, drizzle and urban decay.

'Guerrero Street? Hmm, well, It's pretty complicated. Actually I'm heading up that way though.'

'You want a lift in exchange for directions?' I asked.

'You promise not to hurt me?' she joked.

'I'm English. We're only dangerous when there's footballs involved.' She climbed in and we fell into easy conversation. Her name was Suzy and she worked in City Lights Bookshop, famous for having published Ginsberg's *Howl*. She asked what

I was doing in San Francisco.

'I've come to explore different communities. I'm on a journey in search of Utopia.'

Suzy put her hand over her chest.

'Don't you know, David, Utopia is here in your heart?'

I pulled a face.

'Oh, you've heard that? Do you know the Cockettes then?'

'No.'

'They were a bearded drag queen community in the sixties. They all lived together in Haight Ashbury. They used to drop acid and perform shows at the old Pegasus Theatre downtown. You should look into them – very interesting. I know them pretty well.'

'They're still going?'

'Sort of. A couple of them will be at a party tonight. Wanna come? You have a beautiful accent by the way.'

In England the journey from meeting a stranger to becoming their new best friend is long and arduous. In San Francisco it took ten minutes. And while Suzy's friends from the Cockettes never did materialise at the party that night, I didn't mind. I was soon surrounded by friendly Californians, swooning at my accent.

'Go on, say "cup of tea",' my audience urged.

'Cup of tea.'

'Mmm, sexy voice!' shouted one of the girls. OK, so now I'm revealing my shallow side, but come on – where else but the States would a man born in Scunthorpe and raised in Doncaster enjoy such unwarranted attention?

The following morning, having collected twenty new best friends and a bunch of business cards stuffed in my wallet, I embarked on the long drive southwards down California's Route 101. If driving down this road is not in one of those fifty-things-to-do-before-you're-too-decrepit-type books, then it should be. Route 101 boasts hundreds of miles of stunning coastlines, skeletal cliffs, eucalyptus trees, shimmering ocean, golden sand and serpentine roads. Even the warning sign 'Dangerous curves for the next seventy-four miles', really means 'You are now entering a cinematic car-chase paradise!'. And being California, of course, the sun is always shining.

I drove past Santa Cruz, Monterey and Carmel, which brought to mind images of Clint Eastwood as the unlikely DJ in *Play Misty for Me*, sporting psychedelic shirts and giant collars. My playlist – the Byrds, Love, Alice Coltrane, the Beach Boys' 'Surf's Up' – made the perfect soundtrack to my road trip, with the obvious omission of a certain song by the Eagles.

After nearly two hundred miles I was ready for a break and succumbed to one of the enticing vista stops to watch the sun set over the ocean. A few people were milling around the cliff's edge. A young guy in his late teens wandered over to say hello.

'Hi, I'm John. Want a draw?' he said, offering me a joint. I shook my head.

'I'm driving, don't want to turn up stoned at Esalen.'

'Oh, you're going there? Best way to arrive, man.' He paused. 'Want to hear my latest song? My band are called Radical Nomad.'

Before waiting for a reply John had turned on the car stereo, wound down the windows, climbed onto the roof of his car and began to sing over a backing tape.

During John's 'set' (he sang four songs in total) I struck up a conversation with his father, a retired hippy called Harvey. The pair were travelling up and down the coast on vacation.

'What you doing at Esalen?' he asked.

'Looking for Utopia,' came my stock reply.

'You won't find it there.'

'You're not going to tell me it's in my heart are you?' I said.

'No, man. It's here all around you. In the rocks and trees, the water, the air. Can you smell the eucalyptus? That's Utopia.' John clambered off the car roof and handed me a guitar.

'Want to sing us something?' With a little encouragement I sang 'Pleasant Street', an old Tim Buckley song, proud that my British reserve had loosened its grip as the year went on. I hugged my new best friends, pocketed more business cards and left John and Harvey standing in the dusk, the tips of their cigarettes fading away in my wing mirror. What is it with Americans and business cards? While a slight cynicism was creeping over me that all this friendliness was a thinly-veiled excuse for Americans to advertise themselves, I couldn't help but be charmed by the ease with which conversations took place.

Would such an encounter *ever* take place in a lay-by in England? The only intimacy between strangers I knew about in English lay-bys was dogging. And if you don't know what that is, it's probably for the best.

It was dark by the time I checked in at Esalen Hot Springs. Low lights amongst the bushes and trees guided my way down winding paths, past a multitude of wooden huts, in one of which I found my bed. My roommate was already in his, covers over his head. I could just see wisps of grey hair sticking out from the edge of the blanket. I tiptoed around, trying not to wake him. I needn't have worried. The moment I hit the sack the noises began. I was kept awake most of the night by his hacking cough and frequent trips to the bathroom. By dawn he must have coughed up most of his internal organs. I finally dozed off with the early light and awoke to find the hut empty, just a crumpled hankie and a hat where my neighbour had lain. I never saw him again. He had, I could only conclude, coughed himself out of existence.

Despite the grogginess of a bad night's sleep, stepping out that morning into the warmth of the Californian sun I felt a surge of happiness. Esalen stretched out over several acres of cleared land, set within the redwood forest. Dozens of attractive stone and wood buildings dotting the landscape were used for courses and therapy sessions. In the centre stood the reception, self-service restaurant, swimming pool and, on the edge on the community, an allotment. There was an atmosphere of serenity to the place. Handmade wooden signs bore simple directions: 'To the forest', 'To the restaurant', 'To the ocean'.

As I followed the path from my wooden chalet down the hill, swarms of Monarch butterflies tumbled past me like Woodstock in the Charlie Brown cartoons. Tiny humming birds danced around red flowers. The sweet smell of eucalyptus and campfires hung in the air. Esalen was a verdant paradise.

I reached a large garden and the swimming pool, around which a group of women were doing tai chi. People were lounging around, eating food and chatting. It was a scene of utter contentment. And then I found what I was looking for: a large wooden sign that read: 'To the Hot Springs'. I bounded down the path to find Esalen's famous hot tubs, crouched improbably on the edge of a cliff, overlooking the Pacific.

After showering in a beautiful tiled room, whose glass windows faced directly onto the ocean, I slipped naked into one of the many stone tubs and soaked for an hour in its sulphurous waters, transfixed by the diamonds of light that danced on the blue water, watching the slick, tar-coloured bodies of otters and pods of dolphins far out to sea. I made space for a couple of silver-haired hippies.

'Man, this place is paradise,' one of them said.

'Mmmm,' I murmured in agreement.

*

Esalen had begun life as a hot spring retreat, perched on the cliffs of Big Sur. Owned by the Murphy family since the turn of the century, Esalen really came into prominence in the fifties, made more accessible by the new coastal road and Big Sur's growing reputation as a bohemian hangout, thanks to such writers-in-residence as Jack Kerouac, Lawrence Durrell and Henry Miller.

By the late fifties, the Murphy family decided to hand over the place to their son Michael. Fresh out of college and full of the pioneering spirit of youth, Michael had been inspired by LA's newest resident, Aldous Huxley, who had been touring university campuses talking about the burgeoning hippy movement and saying that the world needed a 'centre for developing human potentialities'. Michael saw this as his calling: he would convert Esalen into a retreat and research centre for the nascent New Age to explore psychotherapy, yoga, meditation, cutting-edge science and Eastern wisdom. There was, however, a snag. While popular with a bohemian crowd by day, come the evening Esalen was overrun by hirsute and violent biker gangs, using the hot tubs for orgies and drug binges. It wasn't clear who actually ran the place: Murphy or the bikers. They wouldn't take kindly to being asked to leave and make way for yoga classes. So Murphy employed a new caretaker: an aspiring writer with a gun fetish and bad attitude, called Hunter S. Thompson. Barely out of his teens, Thompson was fully armed and dangerous, spending his nights drinking heavily and firing tracer bullets into the sky. He was the right man for the job.

After several unsuccessful, life-threatening altercations with the bikers, Thompson and Murphy decided on a full-frontal assault and organised an unlikely posse of locals: the actress Kim Novak and her boyfriend, folk singer Joan Baez and an elderly Henry Miller. Despite having a small pack of Dobermann dogs and an arsenal of weapons between them, they were all secretly terrified, except Thompson, who was stoned out of his skull. Murphy knew that none of the dogs, when push came to shove, had it in them to bite anyone. The dogs did, however, have the horn, and within minutes of being together the two males began fighting over the bitch, letting out ungodly howls and barks that could have been heard in Utah. By the time the posse of armed novelists, actresses and folk singers had approached the hot tubs, the bikers had cleared out, never to return, fleeing the property in the belief they were about to be attacked by a pack of hounds from hell. At least, that's how Esalen's founders like to recount the story.

In its early years, visitors and speakers at Esalen included historian Arnold J. Toynbee, psychologist Abraham Maslow and Aldous Huxley. Grumpy German therapist Fritz Perls turned up (uninvited) and settled himself in, developing his pioneering work in Gestalt therapy. The self-styled philosopher-entertainer and author Alan Watts, with his honeyed English voice, was a huge hit amongst the Californian New Agers; his presence went a long way in helping the place get established. Following on their heels came Stanislav Grof, Buckminster Fuller and author Joseph Campbell, who recorded his ground-breaking *Joseph Campbell and the Power of Myth* documentary TV series there. Courses ran daily, ranging from 'Value Your Psychotic Experience', to 'Interpersonal Intelligence'. By the late sixties, Esalen was so successful that it was having its phones tapped by the sheriff's department.

Over the next two decades, the community was instrumental in introducing yoga, meditation, tai chi and massage to the US, at a time when such practices were considered outlandish and even subversive. It ran encounter groups, workshops and explored such ground-breaking therapies as primal scream. With encounter groups lasting, at times, up to several months, genuine breakthroughs took place, along with the inevitable casualties and occasional suicide.

Critics denounced Esalen as propagating selfishness and individualism, coining the phrase 'the Me Generation' to describe what was seen as rampant narcissism. Supporters exonerated

Murphy for never allowing one teacher or ideology to take over.

By the early eighties, Esalen's reputation had spread so far that a group of high-ranking Russian diplomats visited for the first time. On arrival, they witnessed a great circle of people in a hot tub supporting one person in the middle. The Russians joined in, excited at the communal work they saw going on and soon became regular visitors. It was this moment that marked the beginning of the end of the Cold War. Or at least, that's how Esalen's founders like to recount the story.

*

It was hard at first not try to drink it all down in one gulp, but I soon found my perfect daily routine: a morning soak in the hot tubs before breakfast, another before lunch and then I'd settle there in the evening when the sky swelled under the weight of stars and the Milky Way snaked its thin cloud across the night sky. During the day I took part in yoga classes, trekked through the redwood forests and lingered over great feasts in the food hall. Gently wrinkling away in the hot tubs I conversed with idealistic old hippies, merry pranksters, company directors, LA scriptwriters and even, one afternoon, some of the cast of *Buffy the Vampire Slayer*.

To get the most from Esalen, I'd been advised to sign up to one of the courses. I had to admit that the one I'd picked, 'A Tender Invitation', *had* sounded woolly. When I asked people there about it they said, 'yes, sounds VERY Esalen.'

It was run by David Schiffman, a portly man with a great

hairy belly protruding from his shirt and a big heart. For five days, a group of us hugged, held hands, swayed, sung, hummed and shared our stories. We were taken to the deck of Esalen's original hot tubs (destroyed by a storm in 1998) where Schiffman's companion, Hecase (pronounced *heck-ace*), an elderly man with long white hair in a ponytail, performed a native Indian ritual with us. Arms outstretched, we were doused in the scent of burning white sage and a feathered wing. It should have been the kind of thing I'd run a mile from, but Esalen already had me under its spell.

Inside a stone building we would take one of our group, open up their emotional wounds and put them in the centre of the room, our hands on their shoulders, heart and back, with Schiffman murmuring his sweet words of compassion, never once falling into cliché.

'This is group therapy, Esalen-style,' he would say, his eyes filling with tears.

Amongst the older crowd in the hot tubs, there was much reminiscing about the past. A regular topic of conversation was whether Esalen had grown conservative or not. Back in the sixties and seventies it sounded like nudity, LSD and promiscuity were all part of daily life there.

'Perhaps it is simply the visitors who have become more conservative,' said Hecase.

'Maybe you're right,' another said, 'but once was a time you could come down here late at night and there'd be bodies gyrating all over the place.' From what I experienced the tubs had not entirely thrown off their reputation for amorous encounters. On my first evening, two women had been in a tub with me, one of them complaining about a sore neck.

'Would you like a massage?' said the guy next to her, quickly adding, 'I'm not coming on to you or anything.' I spotted them the following night wrapped in each other's arms in a secluded corner of another tub.

Hecase was something of a bedrock of the Esalen community. A true native of Big Sur, he'd lived all his life in a small house in the hills near Esalen and as a boy had played table tennis with Henry Miller. To me, he was the archetypal wise old man, with whom I took great delight in sitting by the fire in the evenings, listening to his stories.

One afternoon, he took a couple of us on a trail up the creek, dressed as always in his blue spotted neckerchief, hat with feathers, great walking stick and white hair tied tight behind his head. We climbed high up into the forest. The trees bore the scorch marks of a forest fire that had ravaged the landscape some twenty years previously.

'Resilient bastards, redwoods,' Hecase said. We clambered over fallen trees that blocked the river, their trunks eroded smooth by the water to form gentle waterfalls. Woodpeckers hammered away at arboreal carcasses. Blue jays screeched from the canopies and scrub. We reached a hollowed-out redwood hidden behind gorse.

'Medicine tree,' Hecase said. 'I came here years ago to recuperate when I broke some bones.' The tree had been hollowed out all the way to the top by fire. Inside, crystals and a blanket were hung up.

'When the mood takes me I come and sleep inside it. My house is only over there, beyond that patch of trees,' he said, pointing.

'About forty of us live there. We are a tight community. I'm honorary mayor: it was decided in a poker game. We have a town council once in a while. Well, strictly speaking it's a poker game too. But we do talk about what's going on in the community and what needs doing.'

'How do you share the work?' I asked.

'We don't. We discuss what needs doing then do nothing about it. It always seems to just take care of itself.

'I call this tree Boris,' he added, pointing at a particularly tall and gnarled redwood. 'The Esalen people who went up and down this mountain had a name for every tree. They had a spiritual connection to this land. Now we've handed over the spiritual experience to priests, rabbis and doctors. Religions suppress the relationship with spirit because they've turned it into a business. The priest would be out of a job if everyone had spiritual experiences but if you're quiet, spirit will come into you. When I realised this, life got really simple. Any problem I couldn't solve, I'd come here, relax and a solution would come. Be pissed off or angry, and you cut off all lines of communication. Be still, and an answer will come. It works. It just works. I'm a man of the mountains. I give thanks every day for these trees, these animals. I've been living here fifty years and twice I've come face to face with a mountain lion. You know, the thing to never do with a mountain lion is run away.

They've got an imprint in their brain that tells them anything that runs is dinner. You've got to stand your ground. Not an easy thing to do when a lion is eyeballing you. But I stood my ground and I'm here to tell my tale. It's where I got my name in fact. Hecase is derived from my totem, the mountain lion. And besides,' he said, staring off into the middle distance, 'it's a hell of a lot better than Gregory.'

Hecase

Time passed quickly at Esalen, days merged into each other. Like the lotus-eaters in Tennyson's poem, I was cocooned in a soporific spell far away from the concerns of the real world. The place had got into my bones. I knew it couldn't last (it was expensive for a start) but I just didn't want to leave. Like Findhorn and Damanhur, Esalen relied on courses to generate revenue, its outstanding beauty and the hot springs being a large part of its selling point. I wasn't even sure how much it qualified as a community – the overwhelming majority at Esalen were visitors not residents. But I didn't care. As one of its famous guests, George Harrison, said after his visit in the mid-sixties:

'Compared to England it all seems so bloody easy.'

There were no jets screaming overhead like at Findhorn, no Christiania junkies to be wary of, no crazy work ethic like Damanhur or school-disco fumblings like at the Osho commune. Esalen had comfort, beauty and hot tubs. It seemed I had found Utopia in a New Age Californian resort, but perhaps that was the point. I wasn't at a commune, I was actually on holiday.

One night, after a group of us had squeezed into a hot tub to watch a spectacular meteor shower, I sat by the fire with Hecase and told him about my reluctance to leave. He laughed.

'I see it a lot, David, every weekend in fact. The sad faces of people who don't want to go back to their everyday lives and jobs, people who think they've found some kind of paradise. I love this land. It's Utopia for me. But it's my home. It's where

I was born. It's in my bones. You really want to find Utopia? I'll tell you where it is.'

'Please don't tell me Utopia is in my heart,' I said, 'it'll spoil our friendship.'

'That's all chicken shit. Go home. You'll find it there. Utopia is home. You don't need any great quest or life-changing experiences to find a better world. You just start with a gesture and take it from there. Did I tell you my gum-wrapper theory?'

I shook my head.

'You're walking in the forest, you see a gum wrapper? Pick it up. Become an example. You don't have to be holy. That's your first step towards Utopia. Esalen's greatest gift is the people who come here. I've met some incredible people over the years, usually in the hot tubs. Enjoy Esalen's beauty, David, and move on. Don't become a "bliss junkie". Otherwise you might end up like half the old bastards who used to teach here.'

'Why, what happened?'

Hecase gestured at the panorama before us.

'All this beauty and pleasure on tap? Nothing to fight for?' He paused. 'They drank themselves to death.'

The following day I received a mysterious note, a dinner invitationfrom 'Bina'. I had no idea who she (or he) was but, never one to turn down a free dinner, I agreed. As I sat in Esalen's canteen that evening, a beautiful girl with long dark hair and a broad smile came strolling towards me and my jaw dropped. We had met briefly in the video room on the first day. I'd gone there to watch a documentary about Esalen and found her watching *The Matrix* with a guy called Wayne, whom I had taken to be her partner. Bina had been planning her seduction of me from that moment, and I hadn't even noticed. She was a devout Jew who had returned to the US after eight years in the Israeli army.

'I was in charge of thirty soldiers,' she told me. '"Yes commander, no commander", that's all I heard for eight years. Sometimes I'd have to reprimand them in the dark for fear of them seeing me smile. Laugh just once and you're done for. They'll never believe in your authority again.'

The turning point in our conversation came when I mentioned Osho, and then it all came out: Bina was on a quest to explore her sexuality. She wanted to try everything, no holds barred: exhibitionism, voyeurism, fetish, polyamorous relationships, lesbianism, even Englishmen.

'What was the Osho community like? I bet you had fun!'

'Well I did, but to be honest the whole free-love thing is not really my scene.'

She looked disappointed. I didn't want to take the hint. My one-night stand at the Osho community had been fun but ultimately it had still made me yearn for my ex.

After dinner, she suggested we lay stargazing on the meditation tables, then, when it got too cold, we could 'slip into the hot tubs'. An hour later as we soaked naked in the hot tubs I still hadn't made a move. A few people drifted into view and Bina slid over close towards me.

'Perhaps we'd better make out,' she said, 'to keep them out of our hot tub.'

She put her arms around me and began to kiss me tenderly. When the others had gone away, Bina started giggling.

'I'm glad I persisted. I've heard all about that English coolness.'

We remained there for hours, wrinkling away in the waters, kissing and caressing each other until the sun began to rise. Bina took me by the hand and together we tip-toed naked back to her room. It was my first and only night of a passionate sexually-charged affair, a holiday romance that might have lasted longer, had I not checked my emails.

I now understood what my ex had meant in her previous message about 'planning on living a totally new and more fulfilling way of life in Australia'.

She and Dougal had just returned from a 'mind-blowing six-week retreat at an ashram' in the Catskill Mountains of New York. It had been 'such a life-changing experience', she wrote, that with money from Dougal's (irritatingly) rich parents the pair were now planning to buy a hundred and twenty-four acres of rainforest in Northern Queensland, with imminent plans to move there and set up Australia's first Sivananda Ashram. It would be, she concluded, 'our very own Utopia'.

I was pissed off. I had been upstaged by the woman who had prompted my own search for Utopia. There were two possible courses of action:

- Ignore her and carry on at Esalen with the beautiful Bina.
- In an act of pig-headed masochism, spend a month in

one of these ashrams and, if I hated it (which I secretly hoped), have ammunition with which to judge her new lifestyle choice and extinguish my yearnings for her forever.

The next morning I packed my bags and checked out of paradise.

CHAPTER 7

Groundhog Day

*I dreamt that I woke up. It's the oldest
dream of all, and I've just had it.*

From 'The Dream'
A History of the World in 10½ Chapters
Julian Barnes

In Julian Barnes's novel *A History of the World in 10½
Chapters*, the final tale 'The Dream' tells of a man who has
died and gone to heaven. Offered everything imaginable
he starts with sex, golf, shopping, dinner, meeting famous
people and 'not feeling bad.' And while his choice of pleasures
and experiences change over time, after thousands of years
he eventually gets bored: bored with meeting his favourite
foot-ball players, bored with getting a hole in one every time
on the golf course, bored with having everything he wants.
Eventually he chooses annihilation, something, he is told, that
everyone in heaven comes round to asking for eventually.

Barnes's tale has echoes of a *Twilight Zone* episode from

the sixties in which petty criminal, the weasely Mr Valentine, is shot dead after a bungled heist. He wakes to finds himself in the company of a gentleman in a white suit. The courteous gent offers Mr Valentine a dream house, loose women and money. Each day Valentine cleans up at the local casino and takes home the woman of his choice. Like Barnes's unnamed protagonist he too gets bored, complaining to the man in white that he doesn't want to get what he wants *all* the time and could he fix it to maybe let him lose once in a while? He's told that this isn't possible.

'But this is heaven, isn't it?' he complains. 'Surely I can choose how to spend my time?'

'Whatever gave you the idea you were in heaven, Mr Valentine?' the man in white replies. 'This is the other place!'

Earlier in the year, in an act of supreme cowardice, I had rejected the hardship of a monastic retreat in Scotland in favour of the potential pleasures of a free-love community. The sexlessness of an ascetic commune had remained low on my agenda until my ex's latest email.

The ashram stood in the dip of a sixty-acre valley in the soft hills of Auburn, near Sacramento. In its centre stood three large orange-clapboarded houses and a small pond. Nestled into the surrounding slopes of the hills were thirty or so wooden cabins, each the size of a beach hut. But as my taxi pulled into the grounds, I didn't really take any of this in; my eyes were drawn instead to the unlikely spectacle of a burly man dressed entirely in yellow (with matching lemon-yellow woolly hat) yelling and chasing an emu round and round a field. The driver noticed it too. A Texan, with a raspy drawl, he turned around to me and said, dryly,

'I hope you make it through to the other end here, boy. They sure indulge in some weeeeiirrrdd sexual practices by the look of things.' Man and bird disappeared from view as the taxi sped away up the dirt road.

I had surrendered Esalen, its hot tubs and the beautiful Bina to spend a month at a spiritual bootcamp where the day started at 5.30am and simple pleasures (meat, tobacco, alcohol, sex, sugar, coffee, TV, iPods and physical contact) were denied. I followed a sign to reception and wandered into one of the large buildings.

'Welcome to the Yoga Farm,' said a woman dressed in orange. 'Why do we call it a farm? Because we grow souls here.

Here, you must sign this.' She handed me a list of rules to be followed during my stay. They included:

- Do not point feet towards the altar or teachers
- Do not put feet on chanting books
- Leave all wildlife alone
- Modest dress at all times
- No weapons, alcohol, meat, eggs, garlic or onions allowed

'Are you ok with these?' asked the woman in orange.

'Yes,' I replied, fingering the illegal sandwich in my bag like an explosive. Like the nervous Ringo Starr before his trip to India with the Beatles in 1966, I'd stocked up on essentials. In Ringo's case it had been a suitcase of tins of beans, for me it was biscuits and a chicken sandwich. I needn't have worried. Later I would swing between disappointment and relief on discovering that the ashram had a boutique shop that sold cookies, potato chips and Paul Newman chocolate bars.

I was taken to a small wooden hut five minutes' walk from the main buildings, close to the pond. The word 'Happiness' hung on a sign outside. A racoon scurried under my new home, stopping to stare out at me from below the porch. Inside was just a bed and a chest of drawers.

I unpacked, washed, scoffed my sandwich and, despite the ludicrously early hour, curled up in my bed, exhausted at the thought of dragging myself out of bed at the ungodly time of half past five.

*

'*Om nama shiva* five forty-five. *Om nama shiva* five forty-five,' sang the voice. I had slept through the first alarm call of five-thirty. The voice outside my cabin became more insistent, followed by the sound of knuckles on wood and the peal of the bell.

I shuffled out of bed, slipped into my meditation clothes (loose trousers and a sweatshirt) and opened the door. Outside was pitch black. A coldness hung in the air. I headed out towards the faint light of the meditation hall. There seemed to be no one around, but as I crossed the bridge by the pond the hairs on the back of my neck stood on end. I turned around, certain that someone was creeping up on me from behind.

'Hello?' There was silence. I could see little in the darkness but had the sensation of something large and prehistoric watching me. Was I still in the throes of sleepy hallucinations? I walked on towards the meditation hall. Suddenly I received a painful blow to my right shoulder. I was being attacked! I yelled out and turned around to face my attacker. In the dark I could just make out the silhouette of an emu pelting off into the distance.

In the meditation hall people were helping themselves to herbal teas, settling down on cushions and wrapping thick blankets around themselves. At the front of the room was an altar with two large statues of Krishna and Shiva. Hanging on the wall on either side of the altar were black and white photos of the ashram's founders, Swami Sivananda and Swami Vishnudevananda. The photos had been hand-painted, giving the swamis a sickly pallor. Swami Sivananda, with his bald head, smouldering eyes and yellow skin, looked like a cross between Yul Brynner and Homer Simpson. I closed my eyes for the meditation hour and the battle to silence the chattering voice inside my head began.

*

In the early twentieth century, Swami Sivananda rose to fame as a yoga guru, writing over a hundred books on the subject. The first ashram in his name was established by his protégé Swami Vishnudevananda, a yoga teacher with a chubby face and shock of hair working in Montreal. Swami Vishnudevananda had begun to notice that when his students returned from their holidays they looked more worn out, tired and unhealthy than before they left. After accompanying a pupil on vacation he saw why: they were drinking, smoking and eating more than ever, indulging in all the habits they were so keen to curtail through work at the yoga centre. In response, he established the Sivananda Ashram as a resort for mind and body. Now there are dozens dotted around the globe, serving as retreats, monasteries and communities for yoga devotees. The website describes them as 'simple but austere'.

In the sixties, Swami Vishnudevananda earned himself the nickname 'the Flying Swami'. Having acquired a plane, he had it painted in psychedelic patterns. His publicity photo showed him doing headstands on the wing. The swami's plan was to fly over troubled areas and war zones and 'bomb' them with flowers. Flying non-stop from Canada to London one year he picked up Peter Sellers and they flew over Belfast to drop flowers on the city. After they landed the police came to arrest them, but Sellers disarmed the situation by breaking into his own swami character and goose-stepping around until he had the authorities in fits of laughter.

Swami Vishnudevananda's most notorious stunt was in 1983 when he announced he would be flying over the Berlin Wall. Despite repeated warnings he set off one foggy winter's morning, flew under East German radar and by some miracle avoided being shot down. After landing in a field he handed flowers to a startled farmer and asked to be led to the nearest police station. Not knowing what to do, the East German police gave him a cheese sandwich and put him on the first train back to West Germany.

*

The meditation hall was silent, save for the shuffling of bottoms on cushions and the occasional toilet visits of weak-bladdered meditators. I struggled with sleep, my head nodding down to my lap then involuntarily jerking back up with the occasional (and embarrassing) grunt. *Satsang*, as it was called, started and ended the day: a two-hour religious service that mixed meditation, prayer and debate. I had been on meditation retreats before and was familiar with the difficulties of quieting the mind. The mind was, as Swami Sivananda described it: 'a drunk monkey stung by a scorpion'.

Following meditation was the musical interlude known as *kirtan*. Daily chant books were handed out as one swami played the harmonium and another sang lines for us to repeat. Half-way through the routine, tambourines and other percussion instruments were brought round in a basket. I had read that chanting was the easiest, surest and quickest way to quieten the mind: it was certainly the most enjoyable. After chanting came a philosophical discussion with one of the swamis, then two hours of energetic and physically demanding yoga. By 10am I was almost wiped out. My limbs ached, I stank of sweat. Raging hunger carried me through, with the thought of how pleasurable the first meal of the day would be. Warm goo and a sugar-free vegan cookie came as a crushing disappointment. What I would have given for the plate of pancakes and syrup that were just a small part of Esalen's sumptuous breakfast feast. The meals at the ashram were 'deliberately bland' I had read, 'to discourage overeating and avoid tiredness'. But then I remembered the ashram's shop. Thank you, Paul Newman.

The afternoon at the ashram was a mirror of the morning. After brunch I had been sent to rake leaves by the big barn as part of my karmic yoga duties, while the emu skulked around. I kept my distance, the two of us regarding each other with mutual distrust. Occasionally he would wander over to my pile of leaves, give them a good kick, then wander off. In the afternoon these gardening duties began again, followed by two hours of yoga, dinner, then a repeat of satsang. The day began and ended in the hall in darkness, with meditation and prayers. At nine thirty it was over. When my head hit the pillow I was dead to the world.

'Here we eat rabbit food and get up at five thirty in the morning. What is the point?' said Swami Sivarupananda, on the third morning, addressing thirty or so of us residents and visitors sitting cross-legged on the carpet with steaming mugs of herbal tea at our sides. After two nights of solid sleep, the five-thirty bell that morning had not been so painful. I had stayed awake through the meditation and was beginning to find my way around the shifting melodies and time signatures of the chants for kirtan. Sitting quietly, listening to the swami serve up her slab of Hindu philosophy for the day, I felt the sun's rays filling the room, pleased to have been awake through three consecutive sunrises. She continued:

'All we ask is that you follow the experience and explore the results. Go through the pain to find peace. This comes with self-discipline of the mind, body and breath. The more you fantasise, the more you are unhappy. This life is about facing your illusions. Addiction is one way to lose yourself through objects and desires, but it will ultimately lead to your destruction if it goes unchecked. But the principle is right: lose yourself to find yourself. The feeling of love is a sense of belonging. To lose yourself. But love can cause us pain and suffering too. We're likely to withdraw if it's not reciprocated. The problem is not that we don't love but that what we love is imperfect. We will always find fault with the objects of love. In Hinduism we think man is already perfect, he just doesn't realise it yet. To re-connect with that, he must love what is perfect. And that is God.'

*

'We have no idea where he came from,' said one of the swamis one morning over a plate of bitter greens, rice, pulses and un-sweetened dessert that tasted of chipboard. He was pointing at the emu. Les, as I had learned was his name, was staring in through the window, pecking gently at the glass.

'He just turned up one day. It's a mystery.'

'Is there a zoo nearby?'

'Nearest would be San Francisco, about four hundred miles from here. As far as we know no one's reported a missing emu in this neck of the woods. Total mystery. Just arrived a few weeks ago and made himself at home, as if he'd always been here. He's tame enough but he will peck if he doesn't know you. Sri Devo likes to chase him around the grounds every day. It's become something of a ritual for the two of them.'

Despite turning up most days when I was gardening, Les never seemed to consider me anything other than a stranger and therefore worthy of a peck. Mostly he'd peck at my arms. Once he made a stab at my testicles so I picked up a rake and chased him off. I was beginning to understand where Sri Devo's ritual had come from.

From a seeker's perspective, I was enjoying the challenge of life at the ashram. As I'd discovered at other times in my life, when a strict routine is imposed on me, I relax. Like Bill Murray's cynical newsreader in *Groundhog Day*, I was caught

in a strange world of repetition. Nothing was hurried, there was a ritual for everything. When we were winding down after yoga and my belly was crying out for food, I'd have to be patient. I knew that once we lay down to rest at the end we'd still have to give thanks and tidy up in the yoga hall before entering the kitchen to hold hands, bless the food, sing and thank the cooks. As with attunement at Findhorn, I grew to respect these rituals, wondering again if I could carry these experiences into the 'real world'.

The strict routine left little time for other things to get in the way. Showering, checking emails and making phone calls all had to be considered well in advance. The ashram's sole public computer ran at a snail's pace, a problem confounded by the fact it also had the letters 'a' and 's' missing. A few days could go by before I'd finally get to send an email. Reining in my impatience was a huge challenge.

By the end of the second week, while still struggling to quieten my mind and dampen my regrets at having left Bina and Esalen, my mood was beginning to change. Coffee and tobacco withdrawal and the ensuing headaches had long gone. The lightness of food was, on the whole, gratifying rather than unsatisfying and my body felt suppler too. After the first week of yoga classes, the teacher had come to me and said:

'I think we have some issues to work on here, one to one. Tell me, do you work with a computer?' I knew what it was. I slouch. When I played violin in an orchestra the conductor made me sit on a stool because of my bad posture. Now I could sit cross-legged on the floor without cushions, do the 'cow' and almost get myself into a headstand.

Time didn't exactly fly by and with no singing plants, romance or hot tubs to keep me occupied, there was a chance for reflection.

One thing I had come to reflect on was that keeping in touch with my ex was like poking at a sore tooth. One of the reasons for my journey was to move on from her, but in coming to the ashram I was indulging in stupid point-scoring that left me still obsessing about what could have been. In reflecting on the embers of our relationship I'd come to realise something else: the two of us *had* been growing apart during our last two years together. It was something that in the ensuing misery and self-recrimination of the break-up I'd not permitted myself to accept. The ashram was proof of the pudding. For my ex, the world of complementary medicine, yoga and colourful knitwear was something she had thrown herself into with her typical high level of zeal and dedication. I admired her passion, and I had loved her for it. But along with my laziness, it had contributed to driving us apart. Where we might once have had a fun night in with a sausage roll and a *Carry On* film, now my ex preferred to meditate. Almost overnight, parties, live music and pubs became abhorrent to her. Her tastes changed so quickly I couldn't keep up. She'd even wept bitterly on her birthday when, in good faith, I'd organised a treasure hunt with all of our friends. Afterwards she'd said, 'That's the kind of thing you enjoy, not me. You don't understand me at all anymore.' At that moment she may have been right, but it didn't stop me loving her. I knew one thing for certain: the ashram lifestyle may have suited the path she was on now, but I was still missing the everyday pleasures and pitfalls of city life. Coming to the decision that I finally needed to stop torturing myself, I emailed my ex and requested that we end all email communication. I still couldn't help feeling a bit pissed off when she didn't reply.

*

At the Yoga Farm, Swami Sitaramananda was head honcho. She was a round Vietnamese lady with a closely-cropped head of silver hair and a stern matriarchal air. Her sidekick, Swami Sivarupananda, a German with bullfrog eyes, was marginally less severe. The two women were Acharya Swami, the lineage holders of the teachings of Vedanta. They were wrapped in orange, the colour of zeal and fire, for burning away the ego and desires. Dedicating themselves to the path of enlightenment and teaching, they had taken vows of renunciation and celibacy and owned nothing except the robes they were dressed in. I found the air of sobriety around the pair claustrophobic at times. They sat on their small platforms in the meditation room surveying the room with critical eyes during meditation, chastising anyone for fidgeting or moving around. The brahmacharyas (trainee monks dressed in yellow) sat at their feet in reverence. There were faint echoes of the pictures I had seen of the Sublime Ladies with their whips being worshipped by men at the Other World Kingdom, but I thought it perhaps inappropriate to point this out. The two swamis took it in turns to lead the philosophical debates. Swami Sitaramananda sometimes had a way of talking down to us like Reception children. She began sentences, pausing for us to complete them, scolding us if we answered incorrectly.

'Life is illusory, is it not? It is coming and...?'

'Going,' we'd murmur together.

'Going. Good. Absolute universal consciousness is the only reality. That doesn't change. What about you? Are *you* your emotions...?'

'No.'

'No. Good. They change. Pain, pleasure, it's always changing, disappearing. Are we our bodies...?'

'No.'

'No. Good. Our bodies change every three months. Every single cell is replaced. Do we have the same bodies as when we were children?'

'No.'

'No. Of course not.' She paused.

'David, you are on a journey to find Utopia. You must have questions.' She'd spotted me nodding off but I had my question primed. There was much talk of the 'loss of self' in these discussions. I'd been thinking about how Osho had described the orgasm as a fleeting experience of the loss of self, which was why we get so hung up on sex.

'Is it possible to experience loss of self through sex or sexuality?' I asked.

'No.'

That was that dealt with.

Like many Westerners, I had mistakenly understood yoga to be a series of postures and breathing exercises, designed for good health. The ashram taught me that yoga was not all headstands and 'downward dog'; these exercises were only a small part of it. For Hindus, yoga is a way of life, part of a connection with the world through service, meditation, self-inquiry, philosophising, work, exercise and diet, all the elements we were engaged with at the ashram.

'To immerse oneself deep in yoga is to see through the illusion of life to the bliss beyond', Swami Sivananda once wrote. For the swamis at least, the ashram provided a journey to transcend the imperfection of the world to embrace the perfect world of God. It was a Utopia found in the heart, as I'd been endlessly reminded on my travels.

Residents at the ashram took on a variety of roles. There were swamis, work study groups and long-term residents. There were also six or seven brahmacharyas, those in the preparatory stage of becoming a monk. At the ashram they were all white men in their late twenties, dressed in yellow to symbolise consciousness. One of them, Ananda, a handsome man, told me he planned to stay there for one year to ensure that a spiritual path had been carved deep enough to carry it with him throughout the rest of his life, whatever career he happened to take afterwards. Brian, a young musician, had come to escape the excesses of his rock and roll lifestyle but felt uneasy with some of the teachings. He'd strike up loud conversations while we were gardening that even I felt uncomfortable with.

'Man, this is NOT life affirming. I want a life with balls, you know what I'm saying? Hey David, you read any Aleister Crowley, man? Now there's a dude who knows where it's at. Be what thou wilt and all that? Shit, my speed-metal band would not approve of my joining an organised religion!' he said, laughing. But Brian was there because a life with balls had left him with some pretty serious addictions. After a few weeks he appeared calmer, more grounded and at ease with himself.

Satya was the most outspoken of all the brahmacharyas. One morning during satsang, Swami Sivarupananda brought up the eight paths of raja yoga. It was rather like the Ten Commandments. The most contentious was path number four: celibacy.

'Do you want to say something about it, Satya?' the swami asked.

Satya had been at the ashram for nine months. A tall man in his early fifties with a soporific voice, he enjoyed telling me stories of his days in Australia, his polyamorous relationships and experiments with psychotropic plants. It was a novelty sharing such candid conversations with someone at the ashram – most other residents kept themselves to themselves.

'They didn't know how psychotic I was when I first arrived,' Satya confided in me. Certainly I could sense discomfort between Satya and some of the other staff. He reminded me of Carel the Belgian punk. Satya was full of vitality and wanted to shake the place up but at the same time seemed wilfully obtuse and uncooperative with the simplest of things. In response to the question about celibacy he had replied cynically:

'You know I don't agree with it. Ask someone who *believes* in the evils of the loss of semen.'

Another resident spoke up.

'Sexual energy is the most potent in the body. Sex is something we can get addicted to, like sugar or alcohol. The loss of semen makes us weaker, less able to concentrate and can result in premature death. We need to learn to sublimate this energy, transform it into something more powerful still.'

'Good,' said the swami, happy she had got the answer she was looking for. 'Now I'm going to read something from Swami Sivananda's *Bliss*.'

'Not the bit where he describes women as "leather bags of pus, blood, urine, bones and flesh"?' sneered Satya. The swami ignored him and began to read:

'The Buddha said, "a wise man should avoid married life like burning coals…"'

'Oh God,' said Satya, and curled up with his head in his hands. The next day he was gone, having done a moonlight flit to San Francisco.

I had noticed that the swami hadn't contradicted Satya. While Swami Sivananda's sexism had been put down by some of the ashram's residents to the patriarchal times he was brought up in, it didn't fit with the idea of a man who had seen through the illusion of life and its cultural conditioning. It was one of several issues that left me divided over the teachings there.

I could see the positive effects it was having on residents like Brian, who clearly needed to escape his druggy life in LA. Seeing it at its best, the ashram was a sanctuary, a refuge from the excesses of modern life. There was a sobriety to the place however, an absence of intimacy, game-playing, storytelling and mischief. I was missing physical contact, another of the things that were prohibited at the ashram. I had got used to showing affection in the other communities I'd visited. I'd even got over my Northern hang-up about hugging. I was irritated by the idea that conversation was deemed a waste of energy. I loved to talk and hear people's stories, wasn't it another way to build compassion? As the majority of residents at the ashram were committed to the path, opportunities for friendship had not been forthcoming. Focus was on oneself and 'inner work', chatter was discouraged.

Every day the same principles were re-enforced: we were there to escape the illusion of life, to realise that all matter and energy were one. But even if all life *is* illusory (as quantum theory may also be suggesting), then why not at least express a little joy and intimacy, play games and have some fun while we're here? It seemed ironic that the life of the ashram's founder, Swami Vishnudevananda, had been anything but austere and sober. He had jumped in a plane and gone on adventures. Like the restless Satya I missed intimacy, humour, friendship, discourse, culture, variety and people. To find it, Satya had returned to the city.

*

The rains came in late November, three weeks after I arrived at the ashram. Meals were no longer served outside but moved back to the floor space outside the meditation hall. Now treated more like a resident rather than a newcomer, I was no longer immune to the chastisements dished out by the swamis. After gorging myself at the Thanksgiving meal (a welcome treat of turkey, cranberry sauce and ginger dessert) I'd fallen asleep during the music concert that followed. There is only so much pleasure to be gained by listening to a man in white socks and sandals playing a dozen ancient flutes, and I had promptly nodded off, only to be sharply prodded awake by a swami. The previous night I'd had a satsuma thrown at me for snoring during a sitar recital.

On my final morning, I walked up the hill near the swami's house. The warm weather had briefly returned. I sat amongst the dried grass and listened to the distant drill of woodpeckers. I could see them flitting between trees with their red rumps, bobbing flight and rat-a-tat. Gangs of fat game birds clustered under hedges and briers. When disturbed, they exploded with squawks and furious flapping but could barely get their plump bodies off the ground. The sun warmed my face and I felt happy. I could return to one of these ashrams in the future if I felt the need to recharge my batteries, but I felt far too attached to the joys and pains of life to want to spend the rest of my days here. I walked back down the hill, hoping to have one last game of chase with Les but he was nowhere to be seen.

Later that afternoon, one of the brahmacharyas, Durgadey, drove me to a car rental place in Auburn, where one journey ended and another would begin.

'Want to stop for some food?' he asked. 'There's a good health food shop in the mall.'

We stocked up on soya ice cream and wheat and sugar-free cookies, and sat on the wall outside the mall.

'It feels weird coming to these places now,' Durgadey said. 'I get the urge to take my shoes off. It doesn't feel right walking around with shoes on.'

'Are you happy at the ashram?' I asked.

'Very. But you catch me at a good time. It comes and goes. You have to work at it. There are always changes to deal with.'

A wobbly-bellied man wandered past us smoking a fag and wearing a t-shirt with the word 'Geek' on it.

'Well, here it is again. The outside world. Missed it?'

'Yes,' I said.

'Well, most people swing between the extreme experiences of life until they get fed up and come to places like this to find a life on a more even keel. There's no hurry. Enjoy what you enjoy. The path will open up when you've had enough of the ride. Yoga is at the end of the chain, where you come to find God.'

Durgadey's parting words were strikingly different to the ending of the Julian Barnes' story, 'The Dream'. For an atheist, there's nothing but oblivion after all the pleasures of life have been realised. For a theist, the end of the journey is finding God. But while both perspectives have contrary outcomes, they do seem to agree on one fundamental thing: the pursuit of pleasure is not enough to keep us happy.

CHAPTER 8

The Golden City

**San Francisco: forty-nine square
miles surrounded by reality.**

Paul Kanter, Jefferson Airplane

Visit the district of Haight Ashbury today and you may think
that San Francisco never got over the sixties. But the city has
since played a pivotal role in the digital revolution, leading
to an explosion of virtual communities. Craigslist became a
virtual marketplace for exchanging free information, set up
(you guessed it) by a guy called Craig. Tribe, a forerunner to
Meetup and Facebook, led to the creation of thousands of
virtual communities, ranging from 'Mac Obsessives' and
'Polyamorous Perverts' to the 'Aren't Vegans a Pain in the Ass'
tribe, which seemed to generate a huge amount of debate (and
photos of steak dinners). San Francisco's online communities
weren't *just* about casual sex and meat though; in 2004

Couchsurfing.com was also founded there, creating a new and altruistic means of finding accommodation – as I'd already experienced. But perhaps San Francisco's greatest contribution to new ways of sharing is the phenomenon known as Burning Man.

What began in 1986 as a few friends meeting on Baker Beach in San Francisco for the ritual burning of an effigy has since grown into a festival of monumental proportions. Tens of thousands gather each year in late August in the Black Rock Desert of Nevada, in an area covering a radius of seven miles. Burning Man has become an intentional community, a small town that grows organically for a week then dissolves. It is a nucleus of naturists, polyamorists, drug fiends, environmentalists, philanthropists, artists and extroverts. If the Other World Kingdom was once the Disneyland for Perverts, Burning Man is the Disneyland for Seekers. The desert is peppered with effigies, freaky sculptures, art cars straight out of a *Mad Max* film and painted bodies. But as Burning Man grew, its founders chose to outlaw cars as a means of transport. Burners now either walk or cycle across the seven-mile grounds. Surviving the harsh extremities of the desert and self-sufficiency are parts of the experience (as are nudity, painting yourself green, choking on sand, building a sculpture out of beer crates and Brussels sprouts, and getting rather hot).

At Burning Man, citizens are expected to honour civic responsibility and take care of the environment. Stalls flogging festival t-shirts and burgers may be a customary sight at other festivals but here there are none. Money and bartering are rejected in favour of 'gifting', giving to others without expectation of anything in return. A friend from England would later tell me of his adventures setting up a free Martini Bar, serving over a thousand free drinks. When the show is over, the 'town' is dismantled. Burners leave no trace of ever having been there. So you can imagine how much I was kicking myself when, on the day I arrived in California, I found out that I'd missed Burning Man by three days.

I was in San Francisco for a week ostensibly to meet up with a lady called Joani Blank, coordinator for some of the city's co-housing groups, another form of communal living that I was keen to explore.

Like Satya who had fled the ashram, I was also relishing the opportunity for some fun. I had struck gold with my new Couchsurfing companion, who, in keeping with the city's fashion for pseudonyms, called herself Remington. (I never did find out her real name.) Her taste for tribal tattoos, feather boas, weed and polyamory marked her out as a Burning Man aficionado. She was halfway through a law degree as a mature student and had long, thick, blonde hair that smelled faintly, but not unpleasantly, of hay. She also had the habit of whispering to herself, as if in discreet conversation with an invisible friend. In true San Franciscan style a friendship came easily. As did an affair. On the first evening, as I prepared to camp down in the living room, she put her head around the door and announced,

'Sure you could sleep in the lounge, David, but you're

welcome to join me in the bedroom.'

That night, in her Utah drawl, Remington recounted a family history akin to a John Irving novel. Raised by a strict Mormon family, she and her three siblings had fled Salt Lake City in favour of the freedom of San Francisco. Remington was a self-confessed pleasure-seeker and polyamorist. Her favourite word seemed to be 'sin'. There seemed little doubt that Remington took delight in rebelling against her religious upbringing. Her three brothers, all of whom were gay, were equally permissive; the eldest was a rent boy, the youngest was a 'furry'.

'Furry?' I'd asked.

'You know,' she said dryly, 'he likes dressing up as a werewolf and having sex. He's had relationships with coyotes, wolves and bears but he's holding out for a werewolf.' I could only wonder what the family found to talk about at their formal Christmas dinners.

As part of my adventures as a seeker, many years ago I'd once taken part in a silent meditation retreat in Wales. I thought I'd find not speaking for ten days a real challenge (if you knew me, chances are you'd agree), but aside from the relentless farting from all the vegan cuisine, I made it to the end without too many tears. The frustrations came afterwards. During those ten days I'd promised to bring some moderation into my life in the outside world but moments after leaving, all commitments were forgotten. I drove to the nearest town, bought a huge pub lunch, spent the afternoon guzzling beer, booked a B&B and lay on the bed scoffing sweets and masturbating (though not at the same time, that would be weird). Now I was back in San Francisco, the routines of the ashram had fallen to the wayside too. I'd promised myself to wake at dawn to do my yoga and meditation but with Remington as a companion, I'd lost all discipline, meaning I succumbed to the delights of late nights, alcohol, rich food and sex. After a month of austerity I couldn't deny what a pleasure it was to be back in a city and sharing some intimacy with someone again.

Over the next few days, Remington, a consummate host, took me on a sightseeing tour over the Golden Gate Bridge to Sausalito, 'where the rich bastards with boats live'. Later, ascending the cliffs of Ocean Beach on the west coast of the city, we watched a couple below us on the sand with a big camera posing naked for each other. Further along we passed Sutro Baths, once the world's largest indoor swimming pool, long since destroyed by fire. On the façade were pictures of women and moustachioed men in vintage costumes perched on walkways, diving and swimming in these once vast water complexes. Wandering through the remains, we saw a whale far out in the Pacific, its body rising out of the ocean, tail flicking like a sleepy fat man in a hammock swatting flies.

One evening, I was taken to Remington's favourite event: a poetry slam, 'Tourette's Without Regrets', in a shabby theatre in Oakland where we were frisked for firearms at the entrance.

'We got any visitors from out of town tonight?' asked the ginger, motormouthed compère. Happy in the knowledge that as a Brit I wouldn't be booed, I raised my hand. Before I knew it, I'd been chosen as one of the five judges for the evening and been paraded around on stage.

'OK fuckers,' the compère said to the five of us, 'if your genitals could talk, what would they say?'

He handed the mike to me and pointed at my crotch.

'Hello Mum?' I suggested, trying to get into the swing of the compère's dark humour. I saw Remington put her head in her hands.

'Hello Mum?' he said, mimicking my accent. 'Oh, we've got one sick Brit here.'

Poets and rappers were brought to the stage for a freestyle rap event: a minute of high-speed putdowns, San Franciscan style. First up was a young black female rapper in gaudy street-wear and an overweight white guy who looked like he'd turned up in his soiled bedclothes. As the music began he pointed at the black girl:

'You're no slick rapper from the 'hood, your lips are like sun-dried banana slugs.' The audience cheered with delight.

'Well look at you, fat dirty geek, just some flabby Leonardo who sleeps on the street,' his opponent retorted to more peals of laughter. When their minute of racial insults was up, the pair hugged and left the stage and another two rappers strolled on.

'For the sake of the sick Brit in the audience,' the compère said, 'and we all know how fucking uptight the Brits are, I'd like to make it clear that what you hear on stage does not reflect the real respect and love my brothers and sisters here on stage have for each other. IT'S JUST A BIT OF FUN. SO UNCLENCH YOUR ASSHOLE ENGLISHMAN!' The audience roared with laughter.

I made a mental note that, in future, I will never volunteer my nationality at a live event, *wherever* I am in the world.

As well as the city's abundance of self-appointed tribes, its residents enjoyed any excuse for a parade or social gathering – the sillier the better. There was Pee-wee Herman Day, when Paul Reuben's fans dressed as their favourite character and took to the streets to do the Tequila Dance. In the Urban Iditarod, teams of human dog-sleds raced people in shopping trollies through the streets. St Stupid's Day took place on April 1st. Participants marched through the business district at lunchtime led by a figure called Bishop Joey. The so-called Black Heart sculpture in the centre was then ceremoniously covered in knickers and, at the allotted hour, the Sock Exchange would take place where the crowd would throw socks in the air like confetti.

To compensate for my disappointment at missing Burning Man, Remington promised to take me out for Santarchy, which took place in early December. Thousands of residents dressed up as Santas and took to the streets on a drunken rampage. Acquiring my outfit for the day proved tricky but eventually one was borrowed from a friend of Remington's and, suitably attired, we arrived at the secret rendezvous in North Beach.

The streets were already packed with Santas, many already lurching about with brown paper bags in their hands. Accordion Santa was leading a large group with a rousing rendition of Boston's '*More Than a Feeling*', elsewhere there were parties of strap-on Santas, Santas in wrestling masks, thongs, full gorilla costumes, Mexican Santas and, bizarrely, several hundred zombies. One Santa handed out cigarettes to drivers as they tried to navigate their way through a sea of red and white bodies. A camp, shaven-headed cop covered in lipstick kisses was attempting to keep order but spending more of his time having his picture taken with Santa girls hanging onto his uniform and feeding him chocolate. Joining the throng we filed down Lombard Street (the city's steepest road), played Twister in Washington Square and continued towards City Lights Bookshop and the red light district. Santas were filing into sex shops and emerging with paddles, whips and other sex toys. Remington, dragged me into Lusty Lady, a sex workers' cooperative. A sign on the way in read: 'All of our movies are banned in Iran and Texas'.

As we entered a peep show booth, a couple dressed as a pantomime reindeer followed us in, giggling. The screen rolled up to reveal a bare-breasted girl with a Betty Page haircut sat on a stool. She began to laugh.

'Oh my gaahd, I'm missing Santarchy! I completely forgot! You having fun?' she shouted as us.

'Yes!' shouted back two Santas and a reindeer.

'Well, if *I'm* missing Santarchy to be here, you're going to have to perform for ME.'

Two Father Christmases and a giant 'furry' turned to face each other. I was about to experience a taste of free love, California style.

*

Remington had gone away for a few days with one of her long-term lovers. We'd only known each other for three days and six hours and already I could feel a pang of jealousy at the thought of her with somebody else. I was only in San Francisco for a little while – was I not enough for Remington? My ego just couldn't let it go. I was half tempted to get in the car and drive the three hundred miles south to Esalen to see Bina, but I knew that she too had other lovers at the community. How anyone can handle polyamory without becoming an emotional wreck is a mystery.

In the ashram I had missed the myriad delights of the city, and as much as I loved the camaraderie of some of the communities I'd experienced, I was beginning to realise that I was an urbanite at heart. So while Remington was away I took the opportunity to do what I had officially returned to San Francisco to do: meet up with Joani Blank. After learning about the co-housing movement from some of the residents at Esalen, I'd got in touch with Joani and explained that I was exploring different types of communal living. She offered to spend a day with me, showing me round a few of the co-housing communities around San Francisco. Up until then, I hadn't really considered that communal living could ever be integrated into the pace and tumult of the city.

Arriving early at our rendezvous in Berkeley, I wandered through its leafy university campus in brilliant sunshine, past the waterfall where Benjamin Braddock loitered in *The Graduate*, waiting for a sight of his lost love, Elaine. Down Telegraph Avenue I passed stalls selling tie-dye t-shirts, cannabis leaf tobacco tins and Native American dreamcatchers. (I'd now resigned myself to the fact that there really is no escaping this stuff wherever you go.)

I entered a cafe. It was full of students, cramming for exams. A group of young men with side-partings were discussing Keynesian economics while frantic classical music pumped through the cafe's loudspeakers, amplifying the coffee-fuelled fervour. I was finally saved from stimulation overdose by the arrival of a woman with a soft face, grey bob and small yappy dog.

Co-housing began in Denmark in the sixties and slowly spread to other parts of Europe. It didn't reach America until the eighties when a couple of architects, Kathryn McCamant and Charles Durrett, who met in Denmark, wrote a book about it and took the idea back home. The concept was simple: these were self-directed small communities within city centres or suburbs where residents could own their own flats or houses but share communal spaces with their neighbours. In most cases this included a communal kitchen, in which residents would take it in turns to cook each night, a shared laundry space and communal green areas. In living this way, costs were reduced, time was saved (by not having to cook so often) and residents had a greater choice in how their neighbourhood functioned. Some co-housing groups catered exclusively to certain age groups or were women-only, but the majority welcomed all. As an article in *The New York Times* put it: 'Ideal for those who want to own an apartment but don't want to feel lost in an impersonal city.'

Berkeley's co-housing community comprised of fifteen or so cottages and duplexes sat either side of a winding tree-lined path, facing each other. I wanted to have a good nose around the communal spaces with Joani, but being the middle of the day, all the residents were at work and, disappointingly, everywhere was locked. Rather than wait for someone to show up, Joani thought it best to head to Emeryville, a forty-minute drive away. This community consisted of a neighbourhood of twenty or so large yellow identikit houses covering an acre of land. The communal areas included a pool, gymnasium and cinema. They were impressive but did resemble functional rooms in an office building. The residents, a mix of young couples, families and retirees, seemed genuinely happy to be living there. But what wasn't to like? They had their own homes plus a share of facilities that most of us would be unable to afford. And each night they had the choice to take part in a communal meal.

The day ended at Joani's own co-housing group in downtown Oakland: Swan's Community. It was a converted warehouse that a couple of dozen of them had bought, pooling their money to have it specially converted to their needs. It resembled a small tenement building with self-contained flats and several communal spaces: a common room, dining room, kitchen and lounge area, kids room, laundry, workshop space and gym. It was more convivial than the spaces I'd seen at Emeryville. On the fridge hung a list of good and bad things that had happened that week in the community.

The good list read:

'Alyn and Michael cleaned out the dumpster; Talia helped Suzanne water Debbie's plants; Alyn and her son washed several 10th Street windows.'

The bad list included:

'Tools disappearing from the workshop.' Underneath, in a child's handwriting, someone had added: 'alien abductions', a drawing of a UFO and a green man poking out of the top.

I shared a pleasant dinner with Joani and several of the residents, all of whom seemed eager to tell me how much co-housing had changed their lives.

'Highlight for me is our weekly fix of the latest HBO series,' one lady said. 'In the past I'd have sat at home watching it alone. Now Thursday evenings are like a party at my house.

About thirty of us squeeze in.'

'What kind of problems arise?' I asked.

'Decision-making is the hardest factor.' said another. 'It happens slowly. It's consensus voting. All must agree. If there's a problem we ask the person blocking to have the community's best interests at heart. It usually works out for the best.'

'How many communities are there now?'

'North America now has over one hundred and fifty co-housing communities,' Joani chipped in, keen to share her knowledge. 'They're spread across the country from California to New York. It's only a small number but it's growing. In Denmark over five per cent of the population live in co-housing communities now. It's the future.'

We retired to Joani's flat, a short walk from the dining room, along a metal walkway. Noticing the washing up hadn't been done, she apologised and went to take care of it.

'Do you notice how the sink overlooks the common area?' she said. 'The idea of this is to connect with the neighbours. We avoid privacy here,' then quickly added, 'it's there if you want it of course, but we came together for more of a sense of community. We eat together three times a week, work together and look out for each other. It's what I always wanted.'

I sat down in the living room with a hot drink. At our feet, Babu, her dog, appeared to be getting amorous with a Scooby Doo toy.

'Look at my cute dog,' Joani squealed, 'it's the only thing he humps.'

I was beginning to notice a large number of books on sex

and sexuality on the bookshelves of Joani's flat.

'I worked in family planning in the seventies and became a sex counsellor for pre-orgasmic women,' Joani explained.

'Back then, the shops were so sleazy and male-orientated that it occurred to me that San Francisco needed a women's sex shop. That's why I set up Good Vibrations as a clean place to sell sex toys for women. It was the first of its kind.' She reached into a drawer and took out an old metal cylindrical device, bare wires dangling from one end.

'A hundred-year-old vibrator,' she said proudly, passing it to me.

At my feet, Babu continued to hump the toy, his teeth gritted in determination.

The previous day, drunk and dressed as a Santa, I'd been fondled by a couple dressed as a reindeer in a peep show booth. Now I discovered I had spent the day with a 'sex maven', admiring her Victorian vibrators while her randy dog humped Scooby Doo. As a seeker I had finally reached saturation point. Out of the blue, I had an urge to be back home in my own kitchen, wearing my tatty old dressing gown, making myself a Horlicks, and listening to a programme about the history of teapots on Radio 4.

CHAPTER 9

Castles in the Sand

In 1986, cinema-owner Bill Heine became an overnight sensation when he commissioned artist and friend John Buckley to construct a large fibreglass shark crashing into the roof of his terraced house in Oxford. Heine had thrown a party at his new home with the theme: 'What shall I do with this house?' to which Buckley had suggested the shark. In the light of America's bombing of Libya that year, it was meant as a political comment on the phrase 'safe as houses', but equally it had the appearance of a wilful act of Dadaism. The day after its appearance the shark made world news, sparking a heated debate about what we should and shouldn't be allowed to do with our own homes. Heine, vilified and celebrated in equal measure, had sidestepped planning permission for the shark, cheekily claiming afterwards:

'I wasn't aware of any law saying you *couldn't* erect a shark in your roof.' For the next seven years, he battled for its right to remain, refusing Oxford City Council's ridiculous 'compromise' of displaying it in a local swimming pool. It finally took an appeal to the Secretary of State for the Environment, Michael Heseltine, whose spokesman, in an act of supreme understanding, said:

'Any system of control must make some small place for the dynamic, the unexpected, the downright quirky. I therefore recommend that the shark be allowed to remain.'

Heine's house remains an anomaly in England where the real architectural travesties and eyesores appear to be the result of heartless town planning. In 1992, writing about the shark in *The Times*, Bernard Levin said:

'The planning committee of the Oxford City Council ruled that it must come down, giving as the reason that it had been put up without planning permission, or more likely just because it was delightful, innocent, fresh and amusing — all qualities abhorred by such committees.'

In contrast to my own country's rigid planning restrictions, the communities I'd visited so far had displayed an architectural freedom that not only proved to be more sympathetic with their environments but also reflected the eclectic tastes of their residents. Findhorn had been phasing out its caravans with attractive Swiss chalets and homes made from old whisky barrels. In Denmark, Christiania's 'anything goes' housing

policy hadn't resulted in a down-at-heel ghetto but a unique array of homes and workspaces. From the eccentric (a house with a tree growing through the middle) to the stunning (a hexagonal Tudor-style house with a glass ceiling), the anarchist community demonstrated how imaginative people can be when left to their own devices. Since much of Christiania was built by residents who were high as a kite, it is tempting to wonder if the odd joint passed around the table at town planning meetings might not be such a bad idea.

Austrian mystic Rudolph Steiner may have been a man whose ideas ranged from the sublime to the ridiculous, but in one of his more accessible 'manifestos for change', he suggested that every government should have a Minister for Aesthetics to ensure that beauty was not left out of committee-led design. And while beauty may be subjective, it'd take a rare individual to find the brutal designs of our modern schools, supermarkets, shopping centres and factories anything more than functional.

At Damanhur, planning permission would have denied us the Eighth Wonder of the World: the Temples of Humankind. During my visit, the Damanhurians had shared plans for their new project: Bucha, a giant geodesic dome with a glass roof and monorail linking it to the temples. Bucha would house the world's largest esoteric library and an underground conference hall. According to Sunset Butterfly Pineapple, one of its functions would be to invite over world leaders to 'learn how to be human beings again'. I doubted that many world leaders would take up the Damanhurians' kind offer to spend a week underground being re-programmed, but it didn't seem likely to happen anyway. As the community were now unable to employ subterfuge with architectural creations, Bucha had been held up by red tape and bureaucracy for more than seven years with no sign of resolution. As with Heine's shark, 'build and be damned' still seemed to be the best way to get things done.

There was, however, another route open for those with

a utopian vision on a grand scale: to build in a place so in-
hospitable that no one else would care. With this in mind
I had one final community to visit, a place to rival even
Damanhur in its scale and ambition: Arcosanti, the City in
the Desert.

*

Italian architect Paulo Soleri began his monumental experiment in the Arizona Desert in the late sixties, in response to
what he saw as an 'epidemic of suburban sprawl in the US'.
He coined the term 'exurbia', writing: 'the most consuing,
the most wasteful, the most segregating kind of shelter is
epitomised by the city of Phoenix. Once out of the centre we
enter a wilderness of malls, isolated houses and burger joints.
To get from A to B requires longer and longer car journeys,
creating more pollution, more stress and time wasted.'

Soleri saw an over-emphasis on the environment rather
than the city as a mistake. 'Sort out the problems in our cities
and the environment will take care of itself,' was his radical
motto. His solution was Arcosanti: a low-impact city built
on a *mesa*, one of the countless plateaus in Arizona's desert
landscape. Occupying only twenty-five acres amongst the four
thousand that Soleri had purchased, Arcosanti would hold
an optimum population of five thousand living in frugality,
sharing and nurturing a sense of community in the city's
uniquely designed high-density dwellings. There would be no
need for cars inside Arcosanti: everything would be in walking

distance, with nature on the doorstep. Soleri described his process as 'Arcology', the blending of the urban environment with its natural surroundings. *Time* magazine hailed Arcosanti as: 'the most important experiment [in urban architecture] undertaken in our lifetimes'. Eager volunteers for building a new 'super-city' were in great supply and in a short time a number of buildings were erected.

Despite lacking the all-important goatee beard and piercing gaze, Soleri was also something of a mystic on the quiet. On the theme of Utopia he coined the phrase, 'Omega Seed', defining it as a utopian end-point in evolution. 'In nature as an organism evolves,' he explains, 'it increases in complexity and becomes a more compact or miniaturised system. The city is a living organism that must follow the same process. Designed for human intercourse and discourse, the city is our appropriate habitat. We must all live communally. It is a mistake to live alone. We need to learn from each other. Our lesson on the journey towards the omega seed is compassion.'

Soleri believed that congregating in urban environments was a necessary part of our evolution, that proximity to others increased compassion. Looking at it another way, when a city sprawls its 'monstrous belly', in the way Los Angeles has done, a sense of connection is lost. In Europe, this is evident in our suburban and commuter zones. Here, in our desire for status and comfort, we cut ourselves off from others by living in detached houses, distancing ourselves from our neighbours, losing our sense of community and removing opportunities to share.

'Our cities of the future,' Soleri concluded, 'will be integrated ecosystems, dense megastructures that grow their own food and produce their own energy and consciousness.'

Arcosanti seemed to combine the best elements of intentional communities and the city. It was co-housing on a grand scale. Despite its overly academic tone, Soleri's book, *The Urban Ideal*, had become something of a bible to me. He was the closest thing I had to a hero in my search for Utopia. Nearing the end of my adventures, I was finally going to meet the great man.

*

With another epic journey ahead of me I set off early from San Francisco for a fourteen-hour drive into the heart of the Arizona Desert. Remington, with a few free days, had agreed to accompany me. While we had both admitted to having feelings for each other, at the same time we knew it couldn't last. I put on a CD of British comedian John Shuttleworth. Remington instantly took to it, repeating back the idiosyncrasies of his Northern dialogue with great delight.

Keen to make good time, once onto the highway I put my foot down. Within ten minutes I heard a police siren behind me.

'Uh-oh,' said Remington casually, 'you've been busted.'

'Are you aware you were doing a hundred miles an hour?' said the fresh-faced cop, glaring at me.

'He's cute,' said Remington, loud enough for the cop to hear her.

The cop glared at us. Whatever chance I had of being let off had now gone.

'Yes,' I replied.

'And that the limit here is 65.'

'Yes.'

'And that it's raining?'

'Yes.'

'May I see your driving licence?' I handed it to him and he marched back to his vehicle. Three parking tickets and two speeding fines had been clocked up in just six weeks. And four of these weeks had been spent at the Yoga Farm. It hadn't taken long to surrender the gentle pace of the ashram to the pulse of San Francisco. After five minutes, the cop returned to my window and handed me the fine. His demeanour had completely changed, as if he'd had a surprise religious conversion whilst fumbling in the glove compartment.

'Drive carefully,' he said with a broad smile, followed by that infuriating American mantra: 'Have a nice day!' I wondered if I'd told him I was in a hurry because I was in search of Utopia he'd have put his hand on his heart, cleared his throat and said, 'Haven't you heard, Utopia is...' – and I'd have been arrested for assault.

I eased off the speed and settled into the drive. Ahead of us lay an endless vista of grass and flatlands. On the horizon, distant trains cut through the desert, paper chains pulled along an invisible thread. Far in the distance, a power station was lit up like a Christmas tree.

A few hours later the land began to rise. The skyline transformed into the rounded teeth of distant hills. The road was dotted with stubbly bushes, tumbleweeds, squat motels and a tempting sign for a 'ghost town.'

On the outskirts of Barstow on the site of the old Route 66 we picked up a hitchhiker. He was a mature student in his late twenties with a Grateful Dead t-shirt, long matted hair and shades.

'English?' he asked.

'Yes.'

'Nice accent. Mind if I smoke?'

'Sweetheart, it's compulsory,' said Remington.

After a few minutes our companion had skinned up a joint to rival the infamous Camberwell Carrot in *Withnail and I*. He blew great plumes of smoke out of the open window then passed it to Remington and me.

Now look, under normal circumstances I'd never drive stoned. The one time I did was in my twenties and I found myself almost grinding to a halt as my ability to multitask vanished and my nervous girlfriend had to talk me through the necessary sequence of manoeuvres: 'Second gear, indicate, turn left, back to third gear...' But with a straight, empty road ahead and at the gentle insistence of my companion and Remington, I took a few healthy tokes on the joint and passed it back to him. A few minutes later, waves of sweet dizziness began to kick in.

'Jesus, it's strong.'

'California's finest,' he said.

I drove on for another hour, all of us too stoned to speak.

As the sun dipped and the landscape began to change again to hills and scrubland, our companion turned to us and said:

'You heard of the skin walkers?'

'No.'

'The Navajo tell these crazy horror stories about them. They're shape-shifters, carriers of the death powder. They run on their elbows, carrying handfuls of bone dust. Cross a skin walker's path and it'll blow dust in your face and take your soul. Friend of mine swears he was driving on this road a few years ago and sees this thing scuttling in the road. He just put his foot down. Stop and look at these things and you're a dead man.'

The waves of dizziness in my head had now been replaced with paranoia. Remington turned the radio on, both of us welcoming the banal sounds of country and western as a distraction. We dropped the student off in Flagstaff half an hour later, the sky now black and lit with stars. The road was still empty.

A few miles later we passed a van upturned on the side of the road like a dead beetle. Dust was blowing through its open windows. There was nobody inside. Remington and I looked at each other, sharing the same paranoid thoughts.

*

I was prepared to be disappointed by Arcosanti. Sunset Butterfly Pineapple, Damanhur's emissary, had visited Arcosanti the previous year to give a talk about her own community.

When I'd asked, 'Is it beautiful?' she replied:

'Do you like concrete?'

Arcosanti looked like a sixties university campus crossed with a set from an old sci-fi film. A jumble of concrete structures stood amongst long pathways, peppered with conifers and bushes. By the entrance was the largest of all the structures, an open-plan two-storey building with a cafeteria, gift shop and offices. Large round windows offset the drab concrete with stunning views onto the desert scrub and distant hills. In the centre of the 'city' stood a series of domed concrete archways, their interior painted in strips of colour that had long since faded under the desert sun. Accommodation for residents looked a little grim: rows of concrete cube apartments stacked together. Above each entrance thick concrete arms extended outwards like crab pincers, ready to nip. I couldn't begin to imagine how uncomfortably hot or claustrophobic they would get in the height of summer.

Wandering on, we found a small dark games room near the centre of the complex, kitted out with pool and a ping pong table but, judging from the layers of dust, it hadn't been used in a long while. It reminded me of the fly-covered rooms at the Other World Kingdom, unloved and forgotten. Another Westworld.

'Fuck, what a dump,' said Remington. While I didn't want to share her cynicism, I hadn't expected the silence. Despite only having enough space to accommodate a hundred residents, Arcosanti showed no evidence of construction work to enable it to reach Soleri's desired population of five thousand.

We returned to the main building to find someone to talk to and found a friendly tour guide who seemed happy to answer my questions.

'Building has been painfully slow these last twenty years,' she said. 'We're only managing to build one apartment per year.'

It seemed Arcosanti was broke. The guide told us that funding for the entire city came exclusively from the sale of bronze bells, designed by Soleri and sold at the gift shop.

'But surely that's...' I began to say.

'Don't ask. That's Soleri's idea, not ours.'

'Asshole,' muttered Remington under her breath.

'Where can I meet him?' I asked.

'He's not here right now. What day is it? Wednesday? You'll have to wait until Friday.'

'Is he away?'

'No. He only ever comes in on Fridays.'

'He doesn't live here?'

'Good God, no.'

The man who had inspired me with the words: 'we must all live communally' was living alone sixty-five miles from Arcosanti in the middle of nowhere, and driving in once a week to check up on his 'experiment'.

Remington and I paid for a few nights in Arcosanti's Sky Suite. Our room was a spacious and attractive self-contained apartment in wood and brushed concrete, with large round windows that offered glorious views of the desert. It was, we were to discover, in sharp contrast to the living quarters of many of the students and residents holed up in dark, bedsit-style concrete cubes. The rest of the first day was spent wandering round these largely empty structures. In the evening, we got drunk in one of the small concrete apartments with a bunch of depressed architecture students on placement. They were crawling up the walls from boredom and had few kind words to say about Arcosanti's creator.

With another day to wait until we could meet Soleri, Remington suggested we take a trip into the desert. After an hour of sand, stones, bush and scrub we reached Jerome, an old copper-mining settlement with its own 'ghost town'. The fake cacti and promise of a 'real working steam pump' for $20 were enough to keep us away. After perusing the high street's gift shops selling John Wayne fridge magnets and plastic bulldogs riding motorbikes we felt we'd seen all we needed. Remington suggested we carry on to Tuzigoot. She'd read about the remains of an old *pueblo* on the mesa there, an ancient village built by the Sinagua, a community of farmers, artists and traders making great pots and earthenware. Dating from 1000 AD, its limestone buildings had long since collapsed from the tireless efforts of the elements, leaving knee-high walls showing where dining rooms, bedrooms and workrooms once were. The pueblo was a similar size to Arcosanti, with more than a hundred rooms inside its two and three-storey buildings. Once, several hundred people had lived there. Like Arcosanti it was built on marginal land, with everything in walking distance and nature on its doorstep.

'Isn't this just what Arcosanti aspires to be?' said Remington. She'd hit the nail on the head. Consciously or not, Soleri had tapped into a city design that had been established in the desert over a millennium ago.

*

The Arcosanti Residents School of Thought met every Friday morning in the 'Red Room'. The hundred or so community members – a mix of long-term residents and unhappy architecture students – sat on plastic chairs facing the stage. After a few minutes Soleri appeared, dressed in grey sweatshirt and trainers, surprisingly agile for a man in his eighties. His voice, weak with age and still strongly flavoured with Italian, was hard to follow. What I could understand seemed flowery and oblique. He rambled on about what residents could expect when Arcosanti reached its optimum population of five thousand, which baffled me. There were less than a hundred people currently living in Arcosanti and none seemed particularly happy. At the current rate of expansion it would take nearly five thousand years for Soleri to realise his dream. Weren't there more important things for discussion?

After twenty minutes he finished talking and someone waved me to the stage. I had hoped my meeting with him would have been alone, but Soleri had insisted we meet face-to-face in front of the audience. I shook his hand and sat down in the chair next to him, feeling under scrutiny. He struck me as the kind of person who didn't suffer fools gladly, so I opened with a direct question.

'Paulo, it's a privilege to meet you and visit Arcosanti. I've not been here very long – only a few days in fact – but I've been travelling around different communities for nearly a year now, and believe that finding ways to generate finance is a key element to the success and growth of a community. Here I am confused about something. You're talking tonight about wanting to expand the city from a hundred to five thousand people. Am I right in thinking you plan to do this just through the sale of bronze bells? So many discussions I have heard at Arcosanti revolve around lack of money. To realise your dreams should you be focussing on ways to generate more income?'

Paulo looked at me contemptuously and said:

'After only three days here your views are invalid. You are ignorant. I have nothing more to say.' And with that he rose from his chair and walked out. I never saw him again. A girl on the front row stood up and said:

'God, he's so fucking obnoxious.' Another called out:

'Don't take it personally, Englishman, he's an old man but there's no excuse for his rudeness. I think your question was valid. Somebody had to say something. Good on you, man.'

'Yeah!' said another guy, standing up and applauding. I felt like Robin Williams in *Dead Poets Society*.

My moment of glory didn't last long. I felt let down by Soleri. Arcosanti was a brilliant concept, but its creator expected its residents to live in cramped, poor conditions without allowing them to contribute towards its evolution. All the stuff about him 'creating the instruments and the residents writing the music' were hollow words. It reminded me of the stories of how Captain Beefheart had gone about creating his album *Trout Mask Replica*. His band, forced to play for fourteen hours a day, were criticised, denied food and provoked into fights by Beefheart if the music wasn't to his liking. He even berated them for holding their cigarettes 'incorrectly'. Like Beefheart, Soleri's message was clear: it was his creation and he wanted to play overlord.

That evening as Remington and I wandered back to the Sky Suite, I heard my name called out. Up on our roof, a couple of figures were watching the sun set.

'David, is it David?' a silhouette said.

'Yes.'

'Come on up.' The pair introduced themselves. They were a couple of old hippies, Elizabeth and Mark, both sporting grey ponytails, jeans and plaid shirts. Elizabeth said:

'I just wanted to apologise for what happened back there, earlier today. Your comment was timely and deserved a response, but the issues are complex.'

Her husband chipped in:

'He's had offers before from corporations and big companies, but he wants to keep his vision pure. Trouble is, I'm not sure how much he really wants to see this place with five thousand or even a thousand people living here. Soleri built this place, it's his baby. He decides what's what. It's an urban laboratory as he called it. He's the scientist who visits once a week to check up on us and then leaves again.'

I wondered if I'd been too harsh on Soleri. Here were two residents who clearly respected his achievements.

'But how can a community function without being in control of its finances?'

'It's true,' Mark said, then paused. 'But look around, this is why many of us are here.' The sun was setting over the crumpled plateaus of the mountains, diffusing a golden hue over the desert. Far in the distance, the only sign of human life was the twinkling of lights on the freeway. He was right, it was beautiful. But it wasn't enough. With Soleri at the helm, Arcosanti was another community that seemed destined to stagnate. It also brought to mind that old adage: 'Never meet your heroes'.

After Arcosanti I was freewheeling. Deciding to indulge in a little tourism with Remington, we headed for the nearest city, Phoenix. As we entered the city boundaries, it was just as Soleri had described. We drove past mile after mile of lone single-storey buildings: McDonald's, Burger King, Jack In the Box, Arby's, Pizza Hut, Taco Bell, KFC, Wendy's, Del Taco, Subway, Walmart, K-Mart, Checker Tires, Jiffy, PC World, PetSmart, Holiday Inn, Arco, Freedom Fortress, Discount Mattress, Sleep America, In-N-Out Burger, Applebee's and

Wells Fargo. After five miles we turned around and left.

'Ever been to Vegas?' Remington asked.

Several hours later we checked in at the iconic Pink Flamingo Hotel in Las Vegas. In a country where the car was king and no one had to walk more than five metres to get anywhere, it seemed ironic that the walk from the hotel car park to our room took twenty-five minutes. We dragged our bags across the car park, down a lift, through a vast shopping mall into the chasm of the casino itself, out the other side to reception, more lift action and along miles of corridors until we finally arrived at Room 1028.

'Vegas,' Remington mused, 'has gone one step further than Phoenix: it's created exurbia within the walls of its casinos.'

We stayed one night, hopping from one casino to another, but my heart wasn't in it. After the depth of experience in Esalen, the ashram and San Francisco, Vegas's 'ironic' charm quickly began to grate.

We drove on, into the heart of the great desert of Death Valley and spent the night at a motel with a golf course, baffled as to how the hottest place on Earth could keep its grass so green. The puzzle was solved early the following morning when, out looking for coyotes and roadrunners, Remington spotted the motel gardener with a giant can of green spray paint.

Back in San Francisco, we said our goodbyes. I'd grown fond of Remington, despite her annoying habit of calling me 'her little Englishman', I'm nearly six foot, for Christ's sake. She was off for a few days to LA with yet another lover, a 'rock musician'. She wouldn't tell me his name. I guessed he was famous. I had to stop myself googling for bands playing in LA that week, it would have only made things worse. The previous day we had bought a Christmas tree, decorated her flat and shared a final meal. It was a brief taste of being back in a relationship. I'd missed it; that simple connection, feeling wanted by another, sharing experiences. I didn't want to be a nomad any more, having flings; it didn't satisfy my soul.

Fleeing the pain of the end of a fledgling relationship, I left San Francisco and journeyed on, heading north through Napa Valley to yet another community: Harbin Hot Springs, whose thermal waters were said to be a knee-trembling forty-seven degrees Celsius.

CHAPTER 10

Just Your Typical New Age Naked Small-Town Mountain Community

I was back in over-familiar territory. Harbin had hot springs, optional nudity and served up a potpourri of New Age beliefs. Some of the community's population lived in mustard-yellow pods and wigwams in the surrounding hills of a valley. Its message board advertised courses in somatic therapy, inner sanctuary rhythm work, yurt building, Earth-child gardening and rebirthing in 'womb-like settings'. In the communal restaurant, bearded men were talking about the problems of rearing chickens. A man in a woolly hat was discussing his 'cutting-edge research into schizophrenia' with a woman in a short dress decorated with pictures of dolphins.

A woman was dancing alone outside the restaurant as I headed up to the hot springs. I passed men in Om t-shirts and knitted caps, women in tie-dyed robes and crushed velvet. In a candle-lit temple I tiptoed into near-boiling waters with the same trepidation as in the cold waters of the North Sea on childhood holidays at Scarborough. My skin quickly turned lobster red. Any sudden moves were met with a sweet pain. The word SILENCE was written above the baths. The heat and the water enveloped me.

'Hi, can you guess my name?' A woman in her fifties with grey hair had entered the waters. She flashed two fingers at me, then one, then two again.

'Two hundred and twelve?'

She shook her head. Then the penny dropped.

'V-I-V?' I guessed.

'You passed the test!' she sung. 'So tell me, why are you here? Are you single?'

I glanced up at the sign SILENCE above us.

Whispering I said, 'Well, I—'

'Sweetheart, you are in luck finding me. You met Ishvara yet? He's the founder. Of course between you and me I think he blasted himself in the head with acid back in the sixties. Blows hot and cold. I used to be a lesbian, you know. I first came here twenty years ago with an Italian escort but she was so protective and butch. I was the only one wearing a bathing suit in the tubs back then. I'm not a lesbian now and I don't wear clothes in the waters. Without clothes we revert back to being children, don't you think? But look, while you're here you have to meet Omi. She's a fairy woman. A REAL fairy woman. Lives in the woods and... OH MY GOD, sweetheart, you've really scored! There's Lucinda's sacred pipe ceremony on Monday. You must attend that. She's an authentic Native American spirit. I mean, she's Jewish and was brought up in the Bronx, but she is the real deal. In fact she's a shape-shifter. You can look at her in one light and she looks a hundred and fifty. Blink and she seems to be in her early twenties. She is adorable. Really smart. She's juicy AND intelligent. Just right for you. She's doing a PhD on the theme of soul in the community. You seem open, like me, serious but playful. She's like that. She's got these teeny hands and a big ass, such a delicate feminine shape. Now she's not a morning person, you should

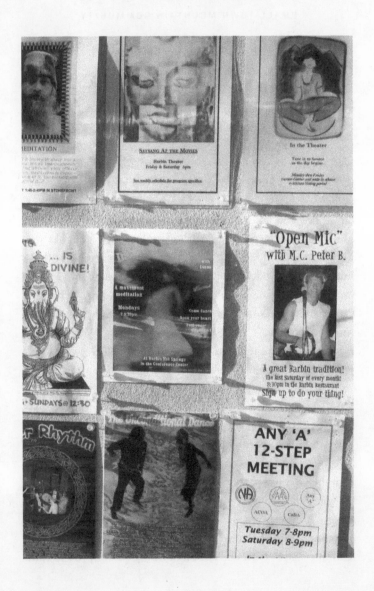

know that. She wears these Buddhist beads in the morning that mean she doesn't want to talk...'

My attention drifted away from Viv's monologue. I had been hoping for some time alone. And then I heard it. A faint sound, coming from an open window. Someone, somewhere, was playing 'Hotel California'.

It was time to go home.

*

A few years ago, I was driving from Brighton to Norfolk for a short break with my ex. We'd rented a one-bed flat and were looking forward to a romantic weekend of sex, walking and drizzle. It was rare for us to venture anticlockwise around the M25 and, as we approached the Dartford Tunnel and the toll booths, my ex began to scramble around the car for coins.

'Shit, I've got no cash, how about you?' she asked. I had nothing either. After rummaging down the backs of the seats and side pockets we'd rustled up 70p. We were 80p short.

'This must happen all the time. They *must* take cards,' I said with misplaced confidence. But as we were pulled into the vortex of queuing vehicles, there didn't seem to be an option for credit cards.

As we reached the toll booth, a woman in her early fifties sat impassive, staring down at me. I rolled down my window.

'I'm sorry but we've only got 70p,' I said, apologetically.

She rolled her eyes. 'Got any Euros?'

'No. Do you take cards?'

'No,' came the deadpan reply. There was a pregnant pause, followed by the horn of the car behind us.

'Can you lend me 80p?' I said, doing my damnedest to be charming.

'No.' Another pregnant pause and more eyeball rolling.

'Erm, so what happens now?'

Her tone turned smug:

'I call my colleague, he will escort you to the next service station cash machine and you will be brought back to pay. It'll take over an hour,' she added.

'But it's only 80p.'

The car behind was beeping again. I felt embarrassed and flustered at holding the traffic up.

A man in a uniform appeared from nowhere and got into the booth with the grumpy woman. He seemed even more pissed off than her. They had a private conference and turned to look at me with contempt. Then I had an idea. Clambering out of the car I approached the vehicle behind me. Scowling, the driver wound down his window.

'Look, I'm so sorry to ask, but we've got no change. I'm sorry we're holding you up.'

His expression changed.

'Oh God, is that all? Sorry for beeping.' He began rummaging around in his coat pocket. To my astonishment the woman at the booth leaned out and began screeching:

'DON'T DO IT. DON'T DO IT, SIR. DON'T GIVE HIM ANY MONEY. *DO NOT GIVE THIS MAN ANY MONEY!*'

Ignoring her, the driver handed me a fiver and said, 'Tell

her we all just want to get home.'

I handed the note to the woman in the booth, who was now apoplectic with rage, and gave the change back to the driver.

As my ex and I drove off, taken aback by what had just happened, we could only conclude that, short of being doo-lally, the woman's reaction was triggered by the dehumanising effect of being cooped up and isolated in a booth every day. It is that same unreasonable anger I see rising up on the road when, trapped in our metal boxes, we are unable to disarm a simple driving mistake with a personal apology and the other driver goes nuts with rage.

Detachment has now become something of a status symbol. We'd like to swap our terrace for a semi and a semi for a detached. If we could afford it, I'm sure many of us would end up living in a mini-fortress with a mile-long drive and a sign outside saying 'Beware of the grizzly bear.'

You're familiar with the scenario, I'm sure. You've got the double seat all to yourself on a train and are feeling pleased but anxious; the train is filling up. Your bag is plonked on the seat next to you in the hope that it'll put off anyone from sitting down. And then it happens: some great oaf spoils your day by lumbering over and asking: 'Is anyone sitting there?' With a look of mild irritation you move your bag and let them sit down. Under normal circumstances, that'd be the end of all conversation between the two of you without the 'unifying experience'. Whether it's a delay, an unexpected attack of the hiccups or a terrible fart emanating from another passenger, something gives you and your neighbour an excuse to speak.

Most of the time these conversations fizzle out but once in a while you get to hear a great story, end up with a new friend or may even acquire a new lover. It's painful to admit it, but that's how my ex met Dougal. This is what can happen when we open our lives to others.

CHAPTER 11

The Quiet Revolution

It was a few days before Christmas. The house was empty. A mound of letters lay on the living room table, put there by a friend who had, heroically, been watering my plants. Among the piles of junk mail lay a handwritten letter from my ex.

My ex had abandoned the idea of the ashram and was now living in Melbourne studying to be an Ecstatic Birther, whatever that was. She had also changed her name. From now on she wanted to be known as Ashamara. Almost as an after-thought she added that she and Dougal had got married. It had been a swanky affair in the Blue Mountains near Sydney, conducted by a Buddhist monk. As a one-off treat, in the evening the newly-weds had 'indulged themselves with a small piece of vegan chocolate cake'.

'Oh, for fuck's sake,' I said out loud.

Was this the same woman I had gone through so many long, dark nights of the soul over?

I still wanted to share with her what I'd been through, to let her know that I'd done it partly for her, but I knew that door was closed for good now.

As I put the letter back on the dining room table, the silence of the house hit me. Unable to bear it I turned on the radio. After a year of sharing my life and living space with others, an empty home had become my idea of dystopia. It was time to throw a party.

*

Over two thousand years ago, Plato's *Republic* was written as a portrait of a model society in which the needs of the individual were balanced with the needs of others, a diorama for how citizens should lead their own lives. I wouldn't have been a model citizen. Like the beleaguered poets, I'd probably have been cast out too. But Plato would probably have despaired at how most of us now live in the West. Increasingly we live and work alone, we litter the streets, play our music loud when others are trying to sleep, urinate in doorways, leave dog shit on pavements and show intolerance for dawdlers, dozy drivers or people in positions of authority. Even my local post office has now felt the need to erect a sign that states: 'Abusive or threatening behaviour towards our members of staff will not be tolerated.' At weekends during the summer, thousands of people come to Brighton to visit the beach. By Sunday evening the amount of detritus from BBQs, picnics and booze-athons would make you think they came to Brighton just to find somewhere to empty their bins.

Obstinately choosing not to follow the news doesn't mean I escape the headlines. I saw one the other day: 'Shamed Britain Must End Loneliness Endured by Elderly'. The news may remind us of the problems of the world, but it offers little salvation. If the news was a Nick Cave song, the headline would be: 'People Ain't No Good'. My hard-line leftie friends would lay the blame entirely on capitalism (and Thatcher), but it runs far deeper than politics.

My parents, like so many of their generation, met at a dance, when dancing was something we did together, intimately and physically. Nowadays on the dance floor, we choose to dance alone. We have driven ourselves to create a society based around individualism, offering greater personal freedom for all, unshackled by the values and mores of the past. But it has come at a price: loneliness, isolation and depression are almost pandemic. In Germany, people now talk of DDR nostalgia. I'm sure few East Germans would want to return to the austere measures of the old communist regime with its state-sanctioned art and crappy Trabant cars, but what they're yearning for is to feel part of something bigger than themselves, a sense of belonging. The twentieth century was full of brutality, war and genocide, committed in the name of political ideologies, many of which, ironically, were triggered by a greater desire for equality and sharing. They all failed. What we have learned is that the desire to share has to be self-directed.

A few months before leaving Brighton, I'd been to visit friends in the country for a soirée. Jem and Sarah, a married couple, were embarking on the middle class dream: they'd bought a huge plot of land and were building their perfect home. They'd waved goodbye to their cramped apartment in the city. No more gardenless abode, noise from the neighbours upstairs and the tiresome daily commute. Their intention was to run workshops and writing retreats from their new home. They had solar panelling, an allotment and were planning to be entirely self-sufficient. With the house still only half-built, guests stood around in its foundations, drinks in hands, looking up at the stars and acres of woodland around, envious of our friends' rural idyll. But halfway through the night Jem sidled up to me, a bit pissed, and said:

'David, I've got to tell someone. We've made a big mistake. It's not what I'd expected. It's so bloody... quiet. Nothing happens out here. I'm bored already. I need to get back into the city, to life, to people. I miss simple stuff like popping out for a coffee in the morning, bumping into friends in town, going for a pint. I'm going stir crazy out here.' Whether they do return remains to be seen. Such stories as this are, of course, legion.

I realise now why it wasn't such a surprise to have kept bumping into Carel in Damanhur. I had joined the alternative lifestyle seekers, hopping from one community to another in search of something different, outside of society. But I struggled with the New Age clichés, incessant bongo playing, inner bliss workshops and the repetitive playlist of hippy anthems. Was there no one out there who liked to wear a vintage suit once in a while, listened to modern music and Radio 4, understood irony and appreciated the genius of Alan Moore? The community circuit came with its own rules, dress code and limitations. But while these communities sprang from ideologies, spiritual beliefs and the stories of crazy visionaries, at their heart was one simple principle missing in city life: an eagerness to share. I shared experiences I will never forget: building Henrik's kitchen, helping to save Nils' life in Damanhur, seeing the Temples of Mankind for the first time, satsang at the ashram, nights by the fire with Hecase and countless hours soaking in hot tubs with people whose stories touched my heart. To me, intentional communities served best as retreats from the excesses of urban life, for soul-searching, self-development and as sanctuaries for those recovering from loss. Had I stuck around at any of them for too long, like my friend Jem in his self-built prison I'd have gone stir crazy too. Both of us had come full circle; a realisation that we needed the vibrancy of the city. For all of its problems, the city, 'designed for human intercourse and discourse' (as Soleri described it) offers a wealth of choice. But still, something needs to change.

As early as the 1920s, some therapists began to talk about how they believed living in communes, villages and small towns was better for our mental health than large, impersonal conurbations. Soleri's solution was to build a new micro-city with consideration for the environment, access to nature, a greater sense of interdependence and close, communal living. But we have to be realistic. Building new cities from scratch isn't going to happen any time soon. Co-housing could be a practical way forward for a greater number to own their own homes, provided they were willing to share communal spaces for laundry, greenery, transport and cooking. In the centre of Brighton is an area called Park Crescent. Over a hundred households, a mix of tenants and home-owners, share a quarter-acre enclosed communal garden. Children are free to roam and play with others. Sure, you might have to put up with some of the kids having names like Wolftone or Chlorella, but what parent wouldn't relish pushing their little ones out of the back door if it came with the knowledge that they wouldn't end up under a car or be catching the first bus to Legoland? Each year, the residents of Park Crescent also hold mini-festivals, fireworks nights and parties. They even have their own community newspaper. But apartments are highly sought after and expensive; when put into practice, people can see the benefits of sharing a large green space. If we pulled down the fences that divide our properties many of us would also gain a communal park. But to get consent to that, first we need to know our neighbours.

*

The kitchen was piled high with food and drink for my Christmas party. Inspired by the creation of Bill Heine's shark house in Oxford, the theme was 'What Shall we do with This

House?' I promised my guests that, like Bill, I'd choose the best idea, no matter how extravagant or bizarre. A huge sheet of paper was erected in the living room and marker pens provided. I was excited to see people scribbling down ideas (and even a Venn diagram) as the evening wore on but, disappointingly, by the end of the night the only idea that was *actually* feasible came from my friend Denise. It was to build a gnome city in my back garden. To get me started she'd even bought me two plastic gnomes.

'Remember, you *did* promise us,' Denise said, in front of the assembled throng.

Halfway through the night another friend, Mark, who lived locally, said,

'Did you hear about Zocalo?' I shook my head. 'I guess you missed it while you were away. It was brilliant. Right up your street.' Since I'd been back, I had noticed Zocalo posters in windows of the local pubs and dozens of houses in the neighbourhood. Put off by the fact that they had been designed with Comic Sans font (I'm a complete font snob) I hadn't given them much attention.

'Loads of people came and sat outside their houses for a few hours,' Mark said, 'it was great fun. Sort of a neighbour day.'

Zocalo, I learned, had been the idea of David Burke, an expat American. David was involved with White Dot, an international campaign to encourage people to watch less telly. Zocalo had been his way of masterminding a mass no-TV day in our area. Instead of telly, people were invited to 'take a chair, sit outside their house and meet their neighbours.' David had flyered the area, knocked on doors, made posters and asked people to spread the word. It had been a great success. Hundreds had taken to the streets, shared food, dragged out sofas and fairy lights and hung out until nightfall. It was so popular that he ran it again a few months later. Here was someone making real social change in my neighbourhood and I'd missed it.

'When's the next one?' I asked Mark.

'Don't know,' he said, 'no one's seen David Burke around for a while now.'

It turned out there would be no more Zocalos. Tragically, David Burke had had kids and moved to the nearby town of Lewes, never to be seen again.

The more I thought about Zocalo, the more brilliant it seemed as a way to encourage neighbourliness in cities. We sometimes had an annual street party in my neighbourhood of Brighton but in the past two years this hadn't happened because of lack of money. Zocalo was free. It wasn't a community event that took months of tedious planning. It didn't require committee meetings or local council approval to close a street. It was an informal street party that could run across an entire city and whose only requirements were a bit of goodwill and owning a chair.

The next morning, sorting through photos from my adventures, I came across one of Hecase from Esalen, sitting in his favourite deckchair. It brought to mind something he'd said to me on our last night together in the hot tubs:

'See a gum wrapper? Pick it up. You just start with a gesture and take it from there. That's your first step towards Utopia.'

'Bollocks to Gnome City,' I thought.

I tracked David Burke down. He was delighted that people were still talking about Zocalo. With my promise of help, he was keen to get it rolling again. Together we set up a website, Facebook group and, on my insistence, had a new poster designed with a hand-drawn font. With the support of a local monthly directory, we got the Zocalo poster set as a full-colour centre-page pullout that was delivered to three thousand houses.

As the day drew nearer, posters started to appear in people's windows again. David and I spent an evening knocking on doors, reminding residents about it. There was a huge amount of goodwill. And, of course, the occasional grumpy sod.

On the day, we strapped a deckchair to the roof of David's car and drove around the neighbourhood making a nuisance of ourselves, blaring Mexican music and yelling out of a megaphone.

'It's Zocalo time!' shouted David, as we rolled up and down the streets. 'You have nothing to fear, good people of Hanover. Step out of your houses. Turn off your TVs. Bring a chair. Bring cakes. Take off your clothes. Run naked in the streets! It's Zocalo Day!'

He might have confused the hell out of anyone who was visiting the neighbourhood for the first time but it seemed to do the trick. At 5pm, like magic, people began to appear on the streets, in ones and twos at first, but pretty soon clusters were gathering. People brought their dinners out to eat, some played games of chess. One family dragged out the entire living

room, complete with oriental rug and bean bags. Kids brought out table football and Jenga to play with passers-by. Elderly residents, wrapped in headscarves and woollens, came out with tea and cakes. David and I strolled up and down the streets chatting with people and taking photographs. After a few hours, I returned to my own street, a cul-de-sac of twelve houses. Many of my neighbours were out, sitting in chairs at the far end of the road. We sat until dark, drinking, chatting and playing music. It was almost as good as being back in the hot tubs.

In case you're wondering, Zocalo is a Mexican word, pronounced *zow-ka-low*. It's the name of the main plazas in Mexican towns and cities where people naturally congregate to spend time together, to indulge in a little hygge, as the Danes would say. In Mexico, as in many other countries, this comes naturally. The Spanish and South Americans have the plaza and the Italians have the piazza – shared spaces for socialising. I realise that, for some readers, I may be preaching to the converted, but in many parts of the world we need to rekindle that sense of neighbourliness. Zocalo served as the perfect excuse many of us need to share a little time with others in our own city.

Nowadays in my street, we have keys to each other's houses. We take it in turns to cat-sit and water each other's plants when we're away. Some of us share a car. One neighbour even built an organic composting box for us all to use. (I do live in Brighton after all.) We also borrow stuff from each other. When it comes to things like DIY tools, does everyone in the

street really need to own one of everything if others are willing to share? Which reminds me, Tim at number ten has had my bass guitar for ages. Tim if you're reading this, can I have it back please? I need it for a gig on Tuesday.

For Zocalo to happen, all it needs is one person in every street or neighbourhood to kick-start a poster or social networking campaign and we're away. No need for fundraising, sponsorship, bureaucracy or political interference. 'Zocalo, Sponsored by Starbucks?' No thanks. If Zocalo were to take off nationally, however, I do fantasise about a time in the future when, through overwhelming public demand, our government would be forced to establish a new national holiday: Zocalo Day, when we'd all have a day off work to plonk a chair outside our house and spend a little time with our neighbours. Of course some folk might not appear to be 'our kind of people' as I had judged my Experience Week group at Findhorn to be, but the simple act of spending time with them and hearing their stories had proven me wrong. And while we can't like everyone we live next door to, we can at least make a little effort to get to know them.

And then there's my own neighbour Tom, who remains as elusive as when I first moved in ten years ago. I chat to him in the street occasionally and put the Zocalo poster through his letterbox, but he never joins in. It's not my place to get all Mao Tse-tung on him; some people really do prefer their privacy. I have to admit though, the strange sawing noises coming from his bedroom last Christmas did give me cause for concern.

The quiet revolution will not be televised. It will not cost any money, be based on hierarchy or exclude a single individual. It will simply be achieved with a chair. And, perhaps, an umbrella. After all, we have to be prepared for a little drizzle some years.

Years ago in Britain, our summer festivals consisted of music stages, fart-inducing cider, mud and toilets that gave you dysentery. Nowadays we have a wealth of so-called 'boutique' festivals. Often set in the grounds of stately homes, they serve up performance art, fancy dress parades, wild swimming, woodland walks, debates, workshops, communal dining experiences and plentiful supplies of loo roll. In a way, they epitomise Soleri's vision of the city: people living communally in high-density frugal homes – i.e. tents (or yurts if you're a bit la-di-da). At festivals there are no barriers to meeting strangers, and they also provide opportunities for mischief and sharing. In the US, Burning Man, with its outsider art, policy of gifting and taking all detritus home, has taken this to another level. But festivals can only ever be temporary Utopias. Afterwards, we return to our cities and the quiet closing of the front door at the end of the day. Christiania, born out of Copenhagen's reserve, is a perennial festival in the centre of the capital, but it remains an anomaly. We need to bring the festival spirit into our daily lives. And it feels like the tide is beginning to turn.

A few months ago, I received an email from a guy called Simon Clare. He was part of a new movement, Sunday Assembly, and asked if I'd like to give a talk about my year away. Sunday Assembly had been conceived by two London-based comedians who wanted to run a new kind of church service. Our churches, they pointed out, were once a great focal point for community. Increasingly many now stand idle. Sunday Assembly brought new life to churches, offering 'the best bits of a service without the Bible-bashing' (many churches are happy to stage these events, as they aren't blasphemous). Their first event included a short reading, an inspiring talk, communal singing, and tea and cake afterwards. It was an instant success, attracting crowds in their hundreds. Before long, Sunday Assemblies were popping up all over the country.

At the Sunday Assembly in Brighton, more than two hundred people turned up. I went with my next-door neighbour, Michelle. A live band was set up near the front of the church and the congregation kicked off by singing 'Girls Just Want to Have Fun' and the theme tune from *Happy Days*. There was a reading from the classic children's book *Pollyanna*, a game that got us all mingling with each other, and then we ended with a rousing rendition of Supergrass's 'Alright'. In the hands of two comedians it could have been flippant and ironic, but our hosts were full of cheeky enthusiasm and at the heart of their enterprise was a sincere desire to share. Like the missionaries of the past, Sunday Assembly's evangelists were about to embark on a world tour to spread the word to Australia, America and beyond, with the promise not to obliterate any indigenous cultures on the way. The will to change how we live in our modern cities seems to be growing.

*

I often get asked if I ever returned to any of the communities I visited after my travels. I have: to Damanhur. It was with my musician friend, Teowa. She often visits to see friends and to give violin recitals inside the Temples of Humankind. On the way over I made the mistake of telling Teowa I was trying to be a 'new man, more giving and thoughtful'.

'Great,' she said, 'then we should put on a concert for the Damanhurians.'

And so it was that I found myself outside the Conference Hall in Crea where, twelve months earlier, I had been part of an unlikely group of Egyptian dancers playing support to a drunken Belgian.

Next door in the conference hall, the host's voice boomed out over the loudspeaker:

'In 1997, Falco talked about how aliens were starting to reincarnate into humans. I wonder if we can discuss this further?' It was just another typical Friday night in Damanhur.

When the discussion had ended, Teowa and I were invited on to the stage to play a few songs for the Damanhurians. Amongst our repertoire Teowa *insisted* we sing 'Hotel California' and 'La Bamba'. Now look, I've given 'Hotel California' a hard time in this book because it's played to death in every community and hostel across the world. 'La Bamba' is another matter entirely. It's a truly loathsome piece of music. But Teowa insisted: these would be the kind of songs the Damanhurians would like. She's not a woman you can easily disagree with.

'After all,' she said, 'who are you doing this for, you or the

Damanhurians?'

She was right of course. The songs *were* well received. The next day we got our pictures in the Damanhurian newspaper and my ego was placated.

CRONACHE

Qui Damanhur quotidiano Giovedì 27 Ottobre XXXI 3

Bravi e simpatici Tea Wa e David

Due musicisti e tanti sorrisi

Ieri sera, come promesso, al termine della serata con Falco c'è stato un piccolo concerto di Teo Wa e il suo amico musicista e scrittore David. Lei suona il violino e lui la chitarra, ma dopo il primo pezzo in realtà i nostri si sono lanciati in alcuni brani divertenti della tradizione musicale degli ultimi decenni, dove lui suonava e lei cantava, un modo inatteso di contattare il pubblico che ha riscosso simpatia e il coro dei presenti per l'ultimo pezzo. Teo Wa ha voluto con questo fare un regalo a Falco e a Damanhur, divertendosi con i damanhuriani.

Teo Wa anche questa volta ha garantito che tornerà presto, afferma che Damanhur le manca e che sarà qui sovente, magari tutti i mesi, per insegnare violino ai bambini delle scuole d'infanzia e elementari damanhuriane...dal canto suo però, dalle voci che circolano, che Jeff Merrifield le abbia promesso che se lo fa veramente, vende la sua auto e le regala una sferoself...vedremo. Anche David si è trovato bene ed ha garantito che tornerà presto. I due partono questa mattina per tornare in Inghilterra.

El.Ge.

Since my first visit, the Damanhurians had created a sequel to their cartoon storybook. As I thumbed through its pages with one of their long-term residents, Mountain Goat, I noticed an image of a giant gorilla wearing shades and a blue scarf, sat in the passenger seat of a car, and then climbing out to swing around the lampposts of Turin. Here was conclusive proof that the Damanhurians really were just having fun, creating a story that they didn't expect the rest of the world to believe. I turned to Mountain Goat. 'Is this meant to represent Gorilla Eucalyptus?' (Gorilla was the hirsute member of the community who claimed to have travelled in time.)

'No,' said Mountain Goat.

'But obviously there was never a real gorilla driving around Turin wearing shades and a scarf?'

Mountain Goat dropped his voice.

'Yes, David. I saw him.'

Not long after my visit, Damanhur's founder, Falco, died. It came as a shock to everyone. Without the man who had set the place up and created its myth, I could only hope that this community, which had worked so hard to resist inertia, would be able to ride the storm.

That same spring saw the death of another visionary: Paulo Soleri. While the world lost a brilliant mind, loosened from the grip of its creator Arcosanti may finally be allowed a little more freedom to grow.

*

Utopia remains a mercurial concept. Some see it as synonymous with God, others, like author Julian Barnes, see it as a reminder of the limits of our imaginations. Despite being conceived as a place of universal happiness, the nuts and bolts of what actually constitutes Utopia remain unique to every single one of us. For some it might be the prison cells of the Other World Kingdom, to others it could be a beach in Thailand. There's probably someone out there for whom it's Skegness.

Christiania was a reminder why most utopian novelists set their communities on an island: to avoid the influence of the outside world. But shouldn't Utopia be inclusive to all? Like the peasant's Utopia in the Land of Cockaigne, for many of us in the West physical comfort and pleasures *are* now immediately to hand, yet abundance clearly isn't enough to make us happy. And if Utopia is a place of peace, why did the Findhorn resident in the hot tub say to me, 'What this place needs is a damn good crisis?' Hecase had spoken about how he'd seen some of the people at Esalen slip into addiction through having too much of the good life. I too had seen family friends retire to an idyllic place in France or Spain and, once the novelty had worn off, quietly slip into alcoholism out of sheer boredom.

The author Colin Wilson wrote: 'Happiness is a sense of purpose'. Perhaps Utopia is a place where we have something important to do, like a project. After all, don't we all need something to struggle for, something bigger than ourselves to make us feel truly alive, whether it's family, friendships, work, a hobby or a cause? Damanhur lived by this principle, setting its residents incredible challenges through building the Temples of Humankind and the Game of Life. Conversely, when the Danes talk of hygge, or the Buddhists of Nirvana, these blissful states are a place *without* purpose.

The Hindus have a word, *lila*, roughly translated as, 'life is a game or play'. In playing games (whether it's chess, hide and seek or Buckaroo) we may enjoy the satisfaction of winning but the feeling is short-lived. We want to play again, we like to be challenged. Much of the pleasure is in the uncertainty of the outcome. Perhaps the very struggle to free ourselves of struggle is, in itself, utopian. If nothing else, Utopia remains a wild land of paradox.

Like Oscar Wilde, I still believe the quest for Utopia remains a meaningful one. For me, it's progress towards a more sharing and compassionate world. But perhaps that's just because that was the journey I happened to need. One of the last conversations I had before the end of my adventures had been with an elderly lady in Harbin Hot Springs, who had drawn up a list of requirements for her Utopia, and found that Harbin fulfilled all of her needs.

'It's really that simple, David. Find a place that has what you want. Or if you like where you live already, whatever's missing you must create for yourself,' she said.

In helping Zocalo to grow, I was making tentative steps. Thanks to Zocalo I had also, unconsciously, fulfilled my special task, as noted by Findhorn's focaliser Daniel at the end of the Transformation Game: 'perform an act of service you can enjoy and do with love for others'. Perhaps, as a newly-improved man, I'm finally ready to progress to a 'Higher Plane'. But before I get too smug and self-satisfied, as my family will attest, having forgotten my sister's birthday again last month, there's clearly more work to be done. But, if I'm honest, there was still something missing. So I asked my illustrator friend Robert Brandt to help me imagine a vision of my own perfect world.

*

Many years ago in Britain, our government made tentative

plans to build 'supercasinos'. How a series of gambling houses would help a nation already struggling with debt was, frankly, baffling. Thankfully, they never took off. But they did give me an idea. To be fair though, it's possible that the Romans had it first.

The prototype for the UK's first Superspa will be on Brighton seafront, close to the pier and with terrific views of the sea. It will be surrounded by lush greenery and peppered with hot tubs made from the discarded beer barrels from Harvey's brewery in nearby Lewes. Nudity at the spa will be compulsory. I know, I know, being British we'd giggle about it for twenty-four hours, but we'd get over it. If I can pull my pants down in a busy swimming complex so can everyone else. And despite Britain's rotten weather, it will be enjoyed all year round. (If you've ever experienced the outdoor spas in Budapest during winter, you'll know what a heartening experience it is to be outside there in the harshest of temperatures.)

Because of the presence of these warm, healing waters, there'll be no opportunity for screens, laptops, mobiles, tablets, iPods or Tamagotchis. Even a humble paperback will be in danger of getting damp. The news will not be shown on a giant plasma screen and there will be no piped music. Unlike a gym, we won't go there for self-improvement but simply to experience a little hygge and share stories with the residents of our beautiful town.

In fact, our Superspa will be a place where great conversations, plans and decisions are made. Even town council meetings will be held there once a month. In the nude of course.

There will be one small snag. People *will* want to flirt. It's only natural. There won't be any point trying to suppress it. To paraphrase Osho: 'if you can't concentrate on the town council meeting because your mind is on sex, then go and have sex'. So I shall have a discreet 'shed' erected at the back for such shenanigans. And while I can't resist an air of flippancy in sharing this vision, if a Superspa existed in my own city, I seriously doubt I'd have ever finished writing this book.

Jean-Paul Sartre famously said 'Hell is other people'. But then he *was* French after all. I prefer to live by the words of Julia in Findhorn:

'There is hope in people. Not systems or governments. Simply in people.'

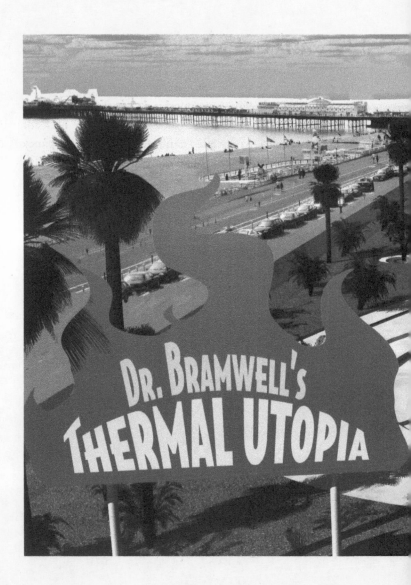

'Somewhere over the rainbow.'

Mark Golding

'Hope.'

Rachel Blackman

'A tolerant society.'

Clive Donnison

'The feeling of peace in the soul from transcending
the self and experiencing the one in all things.
Or some such bollocks.'

Dr Mick Taylor

'Disengaging the mind and being in the now.
Good goddamn, I'm sounding like a hippy.'

Simon Wally

'A bird hide somewhere on the Suffolk coast.'

Carl 'the nose' Vincent

'Love and Magick.'

Sarah Janes

'A bottle of wine, the wife and a
collection of Allen Toussaint tracks.'

Michael Kemp

'No Us and Them Just Us.'

Jason Smart

'Living fully in the present moment.'

Jim Whyte

'The possibility of having no problems.'

Matt Rudkin

'Not a place we strive for but the act of striving itself.'

Tanushak Marah

'No Fear.'

Polly Carter

'Love.'

Donna Close

'Cycling, marzipan and bullet bras.'

Chris Watson

'Freedom and chocolate.'

Emma Papper

**'A place where you are happily in love, surrounded by
friends, where you laugh every day, and are never bored.'**

Kirsty Baggins

'Peace and plenty.'

Aine King

'Doncaster.'

Andrew Stilborn

ACKNOWLEDGEMENTS

A big thank you to everyone at Unbound, especially Rachael, Isobel, Cathy, John and Emily.

Special thank yous are owed to Sadie Mayne, Emma Kilbey, Dippy and Robert Brandt.

SUBSCRIBERS

Unbound is a new kind of publishing house. Our books are funded directly by readers. This was a very popular idea during the late eighteenth and early nineteenth centuries. Now we have revived it for the internet age. It allows authors to write the books they really want to write and readers to support the writing they would most like to see published.

The names listed below are of readers who have pledged their support and made this book happen. If you'd like to join them, visit: www.unbound.co.uk

Mistress Absolute
Ian Alexander
Monty Alfie-Blagg
Peter J. Allen
Georgia Amson-Bradshaw
Martin Andrews
Will Anjos
Simon Appleton
Kirsty Baggins
Charles Baird
Ros Barber
Jenny Barrett
Anna Barzotti
Nigel Berman
Claire Bishop

Judy Blackett
Rachel Blackman
Jane Bom-Bane
William Bonwitt
Gregory Boone
Sue Booth
Corrina Bower
Matthew Bowers
Edward Bowyer
Sue Bradley
Robert Brandt
Dunstan Bruce
David Burke
Philip Burry
James Burt

Cassie Cagwin
Amelia & Hugh Cameron
Daisy Campbell
Xander Cansell
Viv Carbines
Caroline Carter
Sarah Chalmers Page
Claire Chambers
Kayo Chang
Paul Chesson
To Chris with love from
    Sandra – enjoy!
Peter Chrisp
Sarah Chrisp
Mathew Clayton
Kenny Clements
Richard Cohen
Raines Cohen,
    Cohousing Coach
Ady Coles
Stevyn Colgan
John Cooper
Nadia Cooper
Linda Corrin
Cara Courage
John Crawford
Stan Cullimore
Trisha D'Hoker

Jane & Richard Dallaway
Bruce Davenport
Alison Davidson
Brian Davidson
Stuart Davidson
Carole Davies
Melody Davis
Les Dennis
Sam Dixon
Les Dodd
Lawrence T Doyle
Christopher Dudman
Keith Dunbar
Rowena Easton
Charlotte Ellis
Graham Fellows
Suzette Field
Bård Fjukstad
David Flack
Ilana Fox
Jane Gallagher
Susan Gallagher
Beth Gardiner
Lisa Gee
Abbey Gersten
Jo Gibson
Mark Gittins
Sophie Goldsworthy

Terence Gould
Murray Grossmith
Ross Gurney-Randall
Dips Hadfield
Flo Hadfield
Libby Hadfield
Richard Hadfield
David Hadrill
Duncan Hall
Margaret Hallah
Svelte Hardcore
Jane Harding
David Harford
Irene Harris
Peter Hartman
Caitlin Harvey
Peter Hawke
Paul Hawkins
Dave Haygarth
Remo Hertig
E O Higgins
John Patrick Higgins
Tom Hodgkinson
Jason Hook
Andrew Horne
Helen Howe
Peter Huddleston
Robin Hughes

Daniel Hume
Rebecca Hume
Tom Hume
Nevil Hutchinson
Fadi Jameel
Fiona James
Juho Juopperi
Keith Kahn-Harris
Mark Keeble
Andrew Kelly
Michael Kemp
Dan Kieran
Taiki Kimura-Lawson
Teri Kingdon
Fiona Klomp
Leslie Landrey
Kate Lankester
Jimmy Leach
Thibault Lemaitre (@iTibz)
Solange Leon
Diana Linden
George Lloyd
Joy Lo Dico
Penelope Lynch
Katie McCallum
Emilie McDonough
Ewan Mackinnon
Alastair McLellan

Cait MacPhee
Angi Mariani
Ajay Mathur
Catherine Matthews
Sadie Mayne
John Mitchinson
Fiona Mitford
Martin Monteiro
Julia Morris
Nicky Morris
David & Susan Morrison
Claire Morton
Nick Moult
David Mounfield
Helga Munger
Emma Murphy
Al Nicholson
Lauren Nicoll
Wendy Oliver
Bart OToole
Zakaria Outten
Michael Paley
Yianni Papas
Mark Parkinson
Sarah Patmore
Tom Payne
Persephone Pearl

Bella Pender
Monica Perdoni
Abigail Perrow
Langdale Pike
Steve Pike
Tim Pilcher
Alan Pipes
Gordon Pollard
Justin Pollard
Anne Powell
Julian Prior
Tara Pritchard
Adam J Purcell
Jennie Pyatt
Gary Pyke
Catherine Quinn
Susanna Quinn
Katharine Rabson Stark
Julia Rees
Joanne Rich
Rod Rivers
Richard Robinson
Michele Saliman
Steven Saunderson
John Shirlaw
David Shorten
Jinpa Smith

Paul Smithson
Snowy and Whiskers
    (Dips, Jane, Libby
    and Flo's gerbils)
Alexis Soloski
Richard Soundy
Andy Spector
Rita Spencer
Steven StarkStevenS
Andrew Stilborn
Barbara Stocking
Maggie Strasser
David L. Sutcliffe
Susan Tang
Curtis Tappenden
Charlie Taylor
Georgia Taylor
Helen Taylor
Jim Thomas
Gary Thompson
Tjarda Tromp
Elizabeth Van Pelt
Craig Vaughton
Carl Vincent

Natasha Vondervelden
Simon Wallett
Joanna Walsh
Kay Walton
Hugh Warwick
Diana Waters
Fiona Watson
Nicole West
Carina Westling
Diane Weston
The Weston's of Worcester
Ben Whitehouse
Kath Whiting
Carol Whitton
Paul Widdowson
Andrew Wiggins
Will, Jules, Violet & Pebbles
Gaynor Williams
Christine Woodford
Steve Woodward
Rachel Wright
Sara Wright
Lisa Young